Preparing for Sunday

Preparing for Sunday

Exploring the Readings for Year C

J.E. Spicer, CSsR

NOVALIS

© 2003 Novalis, Saint Paul University, Ottawa, Canada

Cover: Suzanne Latourelle
Layout: Richard Proulx

Business Office:
Novalis
49 Front Street East, 2nd Floor
Toronto, Ontario, Canada
M5E 1B3
Phone: 1-877-702-7773 or (416) 363-3303
Fax: 1-877-702-7775 or (416) 363-9409
E-mail: cservice@novalis.ca
www.novalis.ca

National Library of Canada Cataloguing in Publication

Spicer, J. E. (John Ewart), 1919–
    Preparing for Sunday : exploring the readings for
    year C / J.E. Spicer.

ISBN 2-89507-404-6

    1. Bible—Liturgical lessons, English. 2. Church year
meditations.
3. Catholic Church–Prayer-books and devotions–English.
I. Title.

BS390.S66 2003   264'.029   C2003-904928-0

Printed in Canada.

We acknowledge the financial support of the Government
of Canada through the Book Publishing Industry Development Program (BPIDP) for our publishing activities.

Contents

Preface

Near the beginning of my priestly ministry, I gathered groups of people to reflect on our faith. I was amazed at the sense of togetherness that these groups experienced and also at the valuable insights they expressed and shared.

In 1968, Archbishop Jordan asked me to head a new commission in the Archdiocese of Edmonton: Adult Religious Education (a first in Canada). I began by writing reflection booklets on the documents of Vatican II, and then went on to produce bible reflection booklets and guidelines on Mark, Matthew, Luke/Acts, John, and Revelation. These were well received.

More recently, I wrote reflection booklets for all three years of the cycle of Sunday readings. Both groups and individuals in the Archdiocese found these booklets very helpful as they explore their faith.

Preparing for Sunday: Exploring the Readings for Year C grew out of these reflection booklets and will now reach a wider audience. I am convinced that readers' insights, together with those offered here, will lead many people to a deeper appreciation of the great scriptural heritage that is ours.

May God, the Father, Son and Spirit, be with you as you ponder God's word.

J.E. Spicer, CSsR
Edmonton
September 2003

Introduction

How to Use This Resource

Preparing for Sunday is a hands-on, accessible resource for people who wish to explore more deeply the readings for the coming Sunday. Each Sunday lists the readings of the day, offers a brief reflection on the readings and how they relate to our lives today, and ends with four questions.

Begin your reflection time with a prayer. Then read aloud each of the scripture readings listed. After reading my reflection, explore the four questions. If you are part of a group, you may wish to use these "points of departure" to stimulate discussion; if you are using the book on your own, you may simply reflect on the questions or write in a journal. The questions may be reworded or adapted for your setting.

The readings for each Sunday are from the Sunday Lectionary. The Sunday readings are in a three-year cycle (Year A, B and C). Each year of the cycle begins with the first Sunday of Advent and ends with the feast of Christ the King. You will find the readings in a missal or missalette.

Welcome to *Preparing for Sunday*. May the time you spend reflecting on the Word of God bear much fruit!

First Sunday of Advent

Jeremiah 33:14-16
1 Thessalonians 3:12–4:2
Luke 21:25-28, 34-36

The Challenge of Change

In general, we humans resist change. We establish a routine and become comfortable with it. Yet, when we think about it, hasn't our entire life been one of constant change? We all pass through infancy to childhood to adolescence to adulthood. We live in a fast-changing world. Even the Church has gone through many changes.

Will change, then, never end? I'm afraid not, at least in this life. It's simply part of human existence. The more important question is how to live with change, especially in our faith life. Here we need solid direction. We find it in this Sunday's readings.

In the first reading the prophet Jeremiah forecasts that a great change is about to occur: "The days are surely coming...when I will fulfil the promise I made to the house of Israel.... In those days...I will cause a righteous Branch to spring up for David.... In those days Judah will be saved and Jerusalem will live in safety."

In the second reading Paul prays that God will be generous in helping his newly won converts to increase in their love for one another and for the entire world. He then continues, "Finally, brothers and sisters, we ask and urge you in the Lord Jesus that, as you learned from us how you ought to live and to please God…you should do so more and more."

Paul makes clear that we are living out a mystery, the mystery of love, and this challenges us to keep on growing.

The gospel reading focuses on the end of time. "There will be signs in the sun, the moon, and the stars and on the earth distress among nations…. The powers of the heavens will be shaken." This was a traditional way of speaking about end-time. The point is that all the reality we see and feel will be transformed.

Jesus goes on to say, "Then they will see 'the Son of Man coming in a cloud' with power and great glory…. Be alert at all times, praying that you may have the strength to escape all these things that will take place, and to stand before the Son of Man."

Without doubt you and I are people journeying towards end-time. So we are constantly changing, constantly growing. And in this changing and growing Jesus is with us, directing us and urging us on until we attain full growth, full maturity. Now we struggle; then we'll rejoice.

1. Share some of the struggles involved in the changes you've experienced – in your work, for instance, or in other areas of your life.
2. Reflect on the following sayings:
   • "Growth is the only evidence of life." (Cardinal Newman)

- "To change is good. To change often is perfection." (Cardinal Newman)
- "The more things change, the more they are the same." (Alphonse Karr)

3. Share what you see as a comforting presence amid life's changes.
4. What word or phrase from the readings will you carry with you this week?

Second Sunday of Advent

Baruch 5:1-9
Philippians 1:3-6, 8-11
Luke 3:1-6

A New Day Is Dawning

Doggedly we humans journey into the future, hoping against hope that things will improve, that a new day will dawn. But this hope, so deeply rooted, often flickers and sputters in the face of personal troubles and world problems. We may be tempted to give up future hopes and settle for present gain.

It is at these times that we need more than human assurance. We receive it in the readings for this Sunday.

The first reading has to do with the Jewish people who were newly returned to Israel from their exile in Babylon. Things were not as rosy as they had expected them to be. Many times they were tempted to give up the task of rebuilding Jerusalem. But the prophet Baruch speaks out: "Take off the garment of your sorrow and affliction, O Jerusalem, and put on forever the beauty of the glory from God.... for God will show your splendour everywhere under heaven."

Comforting words! They dispel the darkness.

In the second reading Paul says to his Philippian converts: "I am confident of this, that the one who began a good work among you will bring it to completion by the day of Jesus Christ."

The gospel reading begins with a short sketch of secular and religious history leading up to

John the Baptist, for Luke knew that the Baptist heralded a new era in history. He proclaimed the coming of a new and final freedom. Quoting from Isaiah, Luke thus words John's message, "Prepare the way of the Lord.... Every valley shall be filled...rough ways made smooth; and all flesh shall see the salvation of God."

Luke gives us basic assurance about the future. In Jesus, God's plan of salvation takes final shape. In Jesus, the mercy, compassion, power and glory of God shine out as never before. Through the Spirit, Jesus' work continues. God fulfills his promises, and a new and everlasting day dawns in Jesus.

∽⊛∼

1. Share some of your own forebodings about the future.
2. The prophet Baruch revived the flagging spirit of the Jews amid the challenge of rebuilding Jerusalem and the Temple. Apply his words to the challenges you face today.
3. How can Paul's words to the Philippians help us with our personal problems?
4. Reflect on the assurance given us by the gospel reading.

Third Sunday of Advent

Zephaniah 3:14-18a
Philippians 4:4-7
Luke 3:10-18

Come out of Church Smiling

Friedrich Nietzsche (1844–1900), the famous philosopher and a self-confessed atheist, is credited with coining the phrase "the death of God." He is also said to have uttered the following words: "If you Christians would only come out of church smiling I just might become a Christian myself."

Well, Nietzsche may have had a point. Perhaps we should smile more often. Perhaps we don't show our joy as openly and as often as we should. Perhaps the Sunday liturgies should reflect more happiness.

For proof that such a change would be in perfect accord with the best of our Christian tradition, we need look no further than this Sunday's readings.

"Sing aloud, O daughter Zion; shout, O Israel!" So begins the first reading. It continues, "Rejoice and exult with all your heart…. The Lord has taken away the judgments against you…. The king of Israel, the Lord, is in your midst; you shall fear disaster no more."

The second reading emphasizes the same truth. "Rejoice in the Lord always; again I will say, Rejoice," Paul tells the Philippians. He continues, "The Lord is near. Do not worry about anything…."

The gospel opens with John the Baptist telling those who came to him for baptism how they should live. "Whoever has two coats," he says, "must share with anyone who has none; and whoever has food must do likewise."

Some of John's audience thought that he might be the Messiah to come. John knew better. "I baptize you with water; but one who is more powerful than I is coming; I am not worthy to untie the thong of his sandals. He will baptize you with the Holy Spirit and fire."

Now the Holy Spirit is tremendously happy and joyful – infinitely so. Hence we who are baptized in the Holy Spirit ought to do our best to present a smiling countenance to the world.

This doesn't mean being giddy or wearing empty smiles. It does mean, however, that we are not to give way to pessimism, or to a sour attitude towards life. That is not worthy of the Spirit. Deep down, even amid daily worries, we must do our best to be warm, welcoming people.

1. Do the Christians you know give the impression of being joyful people?
2. How can you "rejoice in the Lord" in your daily life, even when you are facing challenges and worries?
3. How can we as a community give more joyful expression to our faith?
4. What word or phrase from the readings will you carry with you this week?

Fourth Sunday of Advent

Micah 5:2-5a
Hebrews 10:5-10
Luke 1:39-45

A Hero to the Rescue

In so many of our daydreams, who plays the hero or heroine? You guessed it: we do. In the nick of time we rescue those in distress. From the jaws of death we restore them to freedom and happiness.

When reality returns, the dream quickly fades. Indeed, a reversal often occurs. We discover that we are the ones in need of rescue. We find ourselves in many prisons, in many suffocating circumstances. What can we do? Is there a way out? Indeed there is. The readings for this fourth Sunday of Advent make that clear.

At the time Micah the prophet lived, Jerusalem was in dire straits. A powerful enemy was knocking at its gates. So Micah cries out to his besieged people: "The Lord says to his people: 'You, O Bethlehem...from you shall come forth for me one who is to rule in Israel.... And he shall stand and feed his flock in the strength of the Lord, in the majesty of the name of the Lord his God.... He shall be the one of peace.'"

Bethlehem was the city of David. So Micah assured the Israelites that a future king of David's line would come in God's name and free them. The first Christians recognized that Micah's prophecy was fulfilled in Jesus.

The second reading, from the letter to the Hebrews, explains how we are rescued. The author places the following words from Psalm 40 on Jesus' lips: "Sacrifices and offerings you have not desired, but a body you have prepared for me; in burnt offerings and sin offerings you have taken no pleasure. Then I said, 'See, God, I have come to do your will, O God.'"

The animal sacrifices of old were unable to accomplish our rescue; something more was needed. And that something more came in the person of Jesus. He came prepared to offer himself as God's obedient servant.

Through obedience to God, Jesus became our redeemer. We, too, are called to be obedient. Mary, the model disciple, shows us the way. Not only did she say in the Annunciation, "Let it be with me according to your word," but in today's gospel she obeys God's angel and visits her cousin Elizabeth.

Elizabeth praised Mary. "Blessed are you among women, and blessed is the fruit of your womb." Through humble obedience to God's word, Mary became the mother of God. And in the same obedience she went to serve her cousin Elizabeth. Elizabeth continued, "And blessed is she who believed that there would be a fulfilment of what was spoken to her by the Lord."

Mary thus makes clear how we are to co-operate in our redemption – by believing in the word of God (Jesus) and being obedient to his command, "Follow me."

~❁~

1. Describe your own heroes or heroines.
2. Why do you think that "obedience" is such a key word for God's people?
3. Reflect upon Mary's example at the Annunciation and in her visit to Elizabeth.
4. How do we discover God's will for us?

Christmas

Mass During the Night

Isaiah 9:2-4, 6-7
Titus 2:11-14
Luke 2:1-16

Mass at Dawn

Isaiah 62:11-12
Titus 3:4-7
Luke 2:15-20

Mass During the Day

Isaiah 52:7-10
Hebrews 1:1-6
John 1:1-18

Events that Shape Our Lives

Sometimes things happen that change the course of our lives. A serious illness or a near-fatal accident. The birth of a first child. The death of a loved one. These and other major events stop us in our tracks and lead us to reassess our lives.

Christmas is just such an event. Though the birth of Christ took place over 2,000 years ago, its true meaning can make us sit up and take notice if we let it!

"The people who walked in darkness have seen a great light.... For a child has been born for us.... His authority shall grow continually." These words of Isaiah were fulfilled in the birth of Jesus.

Paul writes to Titus, "The grace of God has appeared, bringing salvation to all."

And the angel's words in Luke's gospel have the power to stir us to the depth of our being: "I am bringing you good news of great joy for all the people: to you is born this day in the city of David a Saviour, who is the Messiah, the Lord."

Surely the birth of Jesus is a life-shaping event! Indeed, taken together with the rest of his life, and his death and resurrection, it is "the" life-shaping event. Nothing can compare to it.

May the celebration of Jesus' birth renew and deepen our Christian faith, our Christian hope and, above all, our Christian love.

A truly Merry Christmas to all of you.

1. Share your experience of an event that in some way shaped your life.
2. How are people today who have closed their hearts to Jesus "walking in darkness"?
3. Reflect on the opening words of the second reading: "The grace of God has appeared, bringing salvation to all."
4. Share your thoughts on the angel's words to the shepherds: "I am bringing you good news of great joy for all the people."

Holy Family

1 Samuel 1:11, 20-22, 24-28
1 John 3:1-2, 21-24
Luke 2:41-52

Deep Roots

When the wind blows fiercely, only well-rooted trees survive. In the same way, in the often stormy winds of human life, those of us with shallow roots risk being overwhelmed. Popular trends and superficial values are such a strong force.

Christians have a great advantage here, for our faith is rooted deeply in the Old and New Testaments, both of which teach us what it means to be human. Above all, they introduce us to and nourish us in the family of God, as we hear in the readings for this Sunday.

The first reading, from the book of Samuel, tells us how childless Hannah prayed for an heir and was rewarded. She gave birth to a son, Samuel, who in his adult years became both a judge and a prophet. As God's instrument he succeeded in moving Israel from a confederacy of tribes to a monarchy. Only as a monarchy were they able to overcome the Philistines.

In the second reading, John emphasizes the truth that we are indeed "children of God." We are God's family in a special way; thus, our future is assured. As John says, "What we will be has not yet been revealed.... When he is revealed, we will be like him." Our roots are deep indeed!

The gospel records the incident about the young Jesus being lost and eventually being found in the temple, God's house. Jesus then returned to Nazareth with Mary and Joseph and there "increased in wisdom and in years, and in divine and human favour" until in adulthood he brought God's people to ultimate fulfillment through his life, his teachings, and his death and resurrection.

How fortunate we are to be so deeply rooted in God's special family with its long and yet living tradition!

〰❀〰

1. Why do we humans need to be so firmly rooted, especially in a fast-moving age like ours?
2. What values did Mary and Joseph share with their son, Jesus, as he grew up?
3. Through and in Jesus we are indeed "children of God." Reflect on this great privilege.
4. What word or phrase from the readings will you carry with you this week?

Mary, Mother of God (January 1)

Numbers 6:22-27
Galatians 4:4-7
Luke 2:16-21

A Most Special Mother

Down through the ages our human race has had, and has expressed, a great respect and love for mothers. Instinctively we recognize how much we owe to motherly love and care.

But one mother stands out above all others: Mary, the Mother of God. Today we honour her with that title. The readings for this feast help us appreciate the role that Mary, Mother of God and our Mother, plays in our lives.

In the first reading God commands Moses to tell Aaron, the first High Priest, and his descendants in the priesthood to extend a special blessing upon all Israelites. This beautiful blessing reaches its fullness of meaning through Jesus, Mary's Son, the eternal High Priest.

In the second reading, Paul reminds his Galatian converts that Jesus was "born of a woman, born under the law, in order to redeem those who were under the law, so that we might receive adoption as children." As we are adopted children through Jesus (and the Spirit), we are also, in an extended sense, children of Mary.

In the gospel, Luke tells us how the shepherds, following the angels' instructions, went to Bethlehem and found "Mary and Joseph, and the child lying in the manger." As the shepherds returned home, they gave us a clue as to how best to celebrate today's feast. They "returned, glorifying and praising God for all they had heard and seen, as it had been told them."

You and I have been given the same gift. Christ-light has been shining through twenty centuries, as bright now as it was then. Indeed, today it shines even brighter, for the centuries have added to our understanding of Jesus' central place in our lives.

～❀～

1. Some events have a special place in our memory. Describe one memory that means a lot to you.

2. Reflect on Aaron's blessing in the first reading and how Jesus gave it an even greater meaning.

3. We are indeed children of God by adoption. What does this mean in your life?

4. Think about the shepherds' reaction to their visit in Bethlehem. How can we follow their example?

Epiphany

Isaiah 60:1-6
Ephesians 3:2-3a, 5-6
Matthew 2:1-12

Come to the Stable

How often we've said, and heard it said, "That's the last place I thought of looking!" In searching for an item of clothing, or the car keys, or a solution to a problem, we failed to find it. It wasn't in any of the obvious places. Finally it turned up where we least expected.

The solution to the problem of what life is all about is something like that. It's right at hand, only it's found in a less than obvious place – a stable.

In a stable? That's the stumbling block! Who'd ever have thought that the very author of life would choose to breathe his first gasps of air in a lowly manger in a stable? What little light there is in a stable! What poor surroundings! Yet that's the place God chose for the birthplace of his son.

In the first reading Isaiah tells us that "Nations shall come to your light, and kings to the brightness of your dawn." Today, on Epiphany, we celebrate their (and our) coming to the stable of Bethlehem.

In the second reading, Paul assures his Gentile converts at Ephesus that "the Gentiles have become fellow heirs, members of the same body, and sharers in the promise in Christ Jesus through the gospel."

In the gospel King Herod, jealous of the divine infant's power, did all he could to try to kill him. So, too, the powerful of this world seek to squash any power that threatens them.

To find the stable and its immense wealth we must be humble. Like the shepherds, we must listen and then go where God points us.

May we, on this feast of the Epiphany, seek the solution to life's mystery in unlikely places – with the poorest of the poor, with the disadvantaged, with the forgotten, or with sinners and outcasts. That is where Jesus looked.

⌒❀⌒

1. Describe an experience of finding a lost article or the solution to a problem in the most unlikely place.
2. The kings who came to Bethlehem are our ancestors in faith. What does this mean to you?
3. In what ways do you see the divine infant's birth as the solution to life's mystery?
4. What word or phrase from the readings will you carry with you this week?

Baptism of the Lord

Isaiah 40:1-5, 9-11
Titus 2:11-14; 3:4-7
Luke 3:15-16, 21-22

In a Bind

How often we find ourselves in a bind! Sometimes it's our own fault. At other times it's due to circumstances beyond our control. In any case, the binds are bothersome. What to do? One thing we can do is to search the Scriptures.

The readings for this feast day, the Baptism of the Lord, have to do with two big binds: the exile of the Jewish people in Babylon; and the biggest bind, our exile from God because of sin. The way God releases us from this latter bind gives us hope and direction in all the lesser binds in which we find ourselves.

In the first reading, God tells Isaiah the prophet to comfort God's people, for their exile is nearing an end. He is directed to "Speak tenderly to Jerusalem, and cry to her that she has served her term, that her penalty is paid." Then Isaiah goes on to tell how all the obstacles on the way to Jerusalem will be overcome – the valleys filled up, the mountains made low, and rough places smoothed out.

In the second reading Paul assures Titus, and all of us, that "The grace of God has appeared, bringing salvation to all." God's Son, Jesus, "gave himself for us that he might redeem us from all iniquity and purify for himself a people of his own who are zealous for good deeds."

In the gospel Luke tells us how John affirms that he baptizes only with water but that Jesus will baptize "with the Holy Spirit and fire." When Jesus submitted to John's baptism, a voice from heaven said, "You are my Son, the Beloved; with you I am well pleased."

As God delivered the Jewish people from Babylon and, even more wonderfully, all of the human race from sin, surely God will come to our aid in all of the smaller binds in which we find ourselves.

❧❀☙

1. Name some of the binds, small or large, in which you've found yourself (e.g., financial concerns, sickness, problems at work).
2. How is the Jewish exile in Babylon a metaphor for our great exile in sinfulness?
3. Think about John's promise that Jesus will baptize "with the Holy Spirit and fire." What does this mean to you?
4. What word or phrase will you carry with you this week?

Second Sunday in Ordinary Time

Isaiah 62:1-5
I Corinthians 12:4-11
John 2:1-12

Dynasties

History records the rise and fall of many dynasties, both civil and economic. At one time Rome overshadowed the whole Western world. Later on came the Austro-Hungarian Empire, then the British Empire. And the story goes on.

When empires can come and go, is there any solid foundation upon which we can build our lives? Indeed there is, as we see in this Sunday's readings.

The author of the first reading looks upon the newly rebuilt city of Jerusalem around 500 BC and, in God's name, pours out his hope-filled heart: "For Jerusalem's sake I will not rest, until her vindication shines out like the dawn…. You shall be a crown of beauty in the hand of the Lord. …You shall no more be termed 'Forsaken'…but you shall be called 'My Delight Is in Her'…. For as a young man marries a young woman, so shall your builder marry you."

This is powerful imagery! Isaiah recognizes the rebuilt Jerusalem as a symbol of God's undying love for his people, his bride. We are that bride. We are the New Jerusalem.

In the second reading, Paul points out to his Corinthian converts how they are to react to the Spirit in their midst. "There are varieties of gifts, but the same Spirit," he says. "To each is given the manifestation of the Spirit for the common good." He then concludes, "All these are activated by one and the same Spirit, who allots to each one individually just as the Spirit chooses." Each member of the "New Jerusalem" receives the Spirit and is moved to strengthen the community.

The gospel is about a wedding in Cana of Galilee that Jesus and his mother, Mary, attended. Mary noticed that the supply of wine had run out and asked her Son to do something about it. He did so, changing many gallons of water into a wine of high quality, even though, as he said, his "hour has not yet come." But as the time of the cross drew near he said, "Now, my hour has come." Through his cross and resurrection Jesus brought the marriage of God and humanity to its consummation.

Thus, while earthly dynasties come and go, God's dynasty continues on through the ages, growing until at end-time God will be "all-in-all" and we will abide with God forever.

⌒⊛⌒

1. Name some great and small "dynasties" that come and go in our fast-moving world of today.
2. In the first reading Isaiah speaks of a renewed Jerusalem. In what sense does this image of Jerusalem still exist today?
3. In the second reading Paul speaks of the gifts of the Spirit in the Church. How do you see these gifts at work in the world?
4. What does the miracle at Cana say about God's presence and our relationship with God?

Third Sunday in Ordinary Time

Nehemiah 8:1-4a, 5-6, 8-10
1 Corinthians 12:12-30
Luke 1:1-4; 4:14-21

Freedom

Unlike many peoples in our world today, we in the West still enjoy much political freedom. Still, we are not fully free. Many are still hemmed in by injustice or poverty. Others are burdened by financial debts, harmful habits or broken relationships. Hence all of us, in some way, are seekers of freedom.

But in what does true freedom consist? And how do we attain it? The readings for this Sunday offer us valuable clues.

The first reading, from the prophet Nehemiah, concerns the life of the Jewish community newly returned from exile in Babylon (today's Iraq). The people gathered together and asked Ezra the priest to read for them the law of Moses. On the basis of the reading Ezra proposed certain reforms. At this proposal "all the people wept." But Ezra said to them, "Do not be grieved…for the joy of the Lord is your strength." And then Ezra pointed out that such reforms would in the long run bring joy and freedom.

In the second reading, Paul assures us all: "You are the body of Christ." Because we are his body, the risen Christ continues to free us from all that hinders our pilgrimage to God – for in God alone can we be totally free.

In the gospel, Luke presents us with Jesus' opening words of his public ministry. In the synagogue of Nazareth Jesus proclaimed, "The Spirit of the Lord is upon me, because he has anointed me to bring good news to the poor. He has sent me to proclaim release to the captives and recovery of sight to the blind, to let the oppressed go free, to proclaim the year of the Lord's favour."

By these carefully chosen words, based on the prophet Isaiah, Jesus assures us of a new era of freedom filled with the compassion of God, a compassion that accomplishes full restoration to our birthright as children of God.

~❁~

1. Name a few freedom struggles including, if you wish, some of your own.
2. The law of Moses was one step to freedom, but not the last. How did Jesus build on the Mosaic law?
3. How are we the body of Christ?
4. Reflect on Jesus' powerful first words of his public ministry as presented to us in Luke's gospel.

Fourth Sunday in Ordinary Time

Jeremiah 1:4-5, 17-19
1 Corinthians 12:31–13:13
Luke 4:21-30

On Being Rejected

We have all experienced rejection. At some point in our lives, people turn away from us. They avoid us. They no longer talk to us. We are not welcome in their company. A most difficult experience indeed!

But take heart. The first and third readings for this Sunday have to do with rejection. The second reading makes clear how we are to avoid rejecting others and be strong when others reject us.

In the first reading, God assured the prophet Jeremiah of his love while warning him that he will be rejected by those to whom he has been sent. "Before I formed you in the womb, I knew you," God said to Jeremiah. He continues, "I appointed you a prophet to the nations…. Stand up and tell them everything that I command you…. And I for my part have made you today a fortified city…. They will fight against you; but they shall not prevail against you."

Jeremiah prophesied against the many abuses he saw among his people. For that he was soundly snubbed and ruthlessly rejected. Undaunted, he continued to speak out.

The gospel follows upon that of last Sunday, where we heard that Jesus returned to Nazareth for the first time in his public ministry. He read from the prophet Isaiah that God's messenger was sent to bring good news to the people. Jesus then concluded, "Today this scripture has been fulfilled in your hearing."

At first the people of Nazareth acclaimed him. But on second thought they rejected him. "Is not this Joseph's son?" they said. And they went on to criticize him for not working miracles there. Jesus replied, "Truly I tell you, no prophet is accepted in the prophet's hometown." At this all hell broke out – literally! The villagers were set to stone Jesus to death, but he passed through their midst and went on his way (as he would do later in his death and resurrection).

So rejection is common in the lives of those who stand up for God. But the second reading reminds us to continue loving those who reject us with a love that "is not envious or boastful or arrogant or rude." That is the kind of love Jesus expressed on the cross when he prayed, "Father, forgive them; for they do not know what they are doing."

Only love can conquer people who reject those sent by God.

⊷❀↶

1. Share some of your experiences of being rejected when you acted towards others in good conscience.
2. We are all commissioned to speak in God's name. What comfort does Jeremiah give us when our efforts are rebuffed?
3. Reflect on Jesus' being rejected in his own hometown when he claimed to be God's prophet.
4. How is love the basic answer to rejection?

Fifth Sunday in Ordinary Time

Isaiah 6:1-2a, 3-8
1 Corinthians 15:1-11
Luke 5:1-11

Hesitant Pilgrims

In life there are certainly times when we must wait. Nature in general, and many human affairs, cannot be rushed. They need time to mature. On the other hand, there are times when we must speak out forthrightly and act decisively. Otherwise much good would be left undone, or harm caused, by our hesitation.

God has put us into this world for a purpose – to be his partners in drawing all hearts to himself. This calls for decisive speaking or acting when the need arises, as the readings for this Sunday show. To hesitate is to betray our creator.

In the first reading, Isaiah received a vision of God in the heavenly court where the seraphs cry out, "Holy, holy, holy is the Lord of hosts; the whole earth is full of his glory." At this sight Isaiah cried out, "Woe is me! I am lost, for I am a man of unclean lips, and I live among a people of unclean lips."

Then one of the seraphs flew to Isaiah, touched his mouth with a burning coal and said, "Now that this has touched your lips, your guilt has departed." Consequently, when the Lord said, "Whom shall I send?" Isaiah answered, "Here am I; send me!" We, too, are cleansed in Christ and strengthened to act and speak out in his name.

The gospel makes the same point. After Jesus spoke to the crowds on the shore of Lake Gennesaret, he told Peter to go fishing. Peter replied that he had been fishing the entire night and had caught nothing. Jesus ordered him to cast out his nets again. Peter did what Jesus asked and caught so many fish that his boat was on the point of sinking. Thereupon Peter fell at Jesus' feet and said, "Go away from me, Lord, for I am a sinful man!" But Jesus said to him, "Do not be afraid; from now on you will be catching people."

The lesson is clear. Though we are weak, we must never hesitate to act or speak for Christ. Our lips are cleansed in baptism and through confirmation we are sent to speak and act in Christ's name.

In the second reading, Paul speaks to his Corinthian converts about Jesus' resurrection and reminds them that he himself saw the risen Christ, after which he forthrightly spoke and acted in Christ's name. So can we!

1. Recall an experience you've had waiting to speak or act at an opportune time and then doing so (or not doing so).
2. Reflect on Isaiah's experience in the first reading. How does it apply to us?
3. What lesson(s) do you draw from the gospel?
4. What does the resurrection have to do with our speaking and acting in Jesus' name?

Sixth Sunday in Ordinary Time

Jeremiah 17:5-8
1 Corinthians 15:12, 16-20
Luke 6:17, 20-26

In Whom to Trust?

You have money to invest. Whom should you trust? You are launching a new enterprise and need people to help you carry it out, people with expertise, people who will stick with it and not be easily discouraged. Whom do you choose? You need advice. To whom should you go?

These, and many similar situations, frequently surface in the course of our lives. But what of our eternal welfare? Whom should we trust in such an all-important matter? This question is at the heart of this Sunday's reading.

In the first reading, Jeremiah pulls no punches. "Thus says the Lord: 'Cursed are those who trust in mere mortals.... Blessed are those who trust in the Lord.... They shall be like a tree planted by water.'"

In the second reading, Paul touches on the very foundation of the Christian faith – the resurrection of Christ. Without hesitation, Paul answers those Corinthians who contended that there was no resurrection of the dead. "For if the dead are not raised, then Christ has not been raised. If Christ has not been raised, your faith is futile and you are still in your sins."

In the gospel, Luke records four beatitudes (blessings) that Jesus promises to those who believe. He then adds four woes that Jesus addresses to those who put their trust in earthly treasures. Luke thus makes clear that Jesus is the one to trust with our eternal destiny. He knows the way.

1. Describe a time when you were searching for people (or institutions) in whom to put your trust.
2. What do you think was in Jeremiah's mind as he quoted God's curse on those who trust in mere mortals?
3. Why is the resurrection of Jesus the very foundation of our Christian faith?
4. Share your thoughts on the beatitudes and woes as Luke presents them.

Seventh Sunday in Ordinary Time

1 Samuel 26: 2, 7-9, 12-13, 22-25
1 Corinthians 15:45-50
Luke 6:27-38

Making Friends of Enemies

All too often, and in many and varied ways, we make enemies. We don't really intend to, but it turns out that way. What can we do to avoid this situation? The readings for this Sunday point the way.

In the first reading we find King Saul on his way to capture and kill David. David was fast proving to be a great warrior, and therefore a threat to Saul. Yet David had no designs on Saul's kingship. Indeed, when the opportunity to kill Saul arose, David spared his life. To David, Saul was God's anointed one.

David's sparing of Saul's life won Saul over as nothing else could have done. That is why Saul said, "Blessed be you, my son David! You will do many things and will succeed in them."

In the gospel, Jesus speaks out about enemies in the plainest of language, saying, "Love your enemies, do good to those who hate you, bless those who curse you, pray for those who abuse you." He goes on to explain in more detail that love is the only way to win over enemies, concluding with the truth that God "is kind to the ungrateful and the wicked. Be merciful, just as your Father is merciful."

The second reading, at first glance, has little to do with loving our enemies. If we take a second look, however, we see that it does. Paul tells the Corinthians that we are all children of Adam, physically descending from him. But Adam is of the earth. Jesus is from heaven. Through Jesus, then, we are enabled to live a much higher life than as descendants of Adam. All people are related to us both in Adam and in Jesus, and thus they merit our love, for we are all children of God.

1. Share a story (yours or someone else's) of winning over an enemy.
2. Reflect on why David spared Saul's life.
3. Contrast Adam, "a living being," with Jesus, "a life-giving spirit." How are we descendants of both?
4 How does the second reading help us make friends with our enemies?

Eighth Sunday in Ordinary Time

Sirach 27:4-7
1 Corinthians 15:54-58
Luke 6:39-45

The Acid Test

The term "acid test" comes from the chemical analysis of a material object in order to determine its component parts. Now, by extension, it can also refer to tests that determine the stuff of our human characters. When tried under difficult circumstances, we show our true colours.

An understanding of this acid test helps us appreciate this Sunday's readings more fully.

The first reading is from Sirach, a book written a few centuries before Christ. It belongs to a class of writings called "wisdom literature." In this reading, the author makes clear that our true character shows up when we are tested. When the sieve is shaken, the wheat is separated from the lighter chaff. The fire of a kiln brings out any weakness that may be in the clay. The same is true of us.

The gospel is a parable that Jesus told to exemplify how difficult it is to know our inner selves. But unless we do know ourselves, how can we help others? The blind cannot lead the blind.

It takes an acid test, a critical juncture in our lives, to discover our true selves and so be better able to help others.

Death is the ultimate test we face. But Paul assures the Corinthians in today's second reading that "Death has been swallowed up in victory." Through and in the death of Jesus, death has lost its sting. Paul concludes from this victory that our own efforts, feeble as they may seem, are never in vain. Through Jesus we can all pass the acid tests of life.

1. Give some examples of people succeeding or failing in "acid tests."
2. Why, as Sirach attests, does our speech show up our character?
3. What does the parable in today's gospel have to do with acid tests?
4. What help does Paul give us in this Sunday's readings in terms of passing the acid test of death?

Ninth Sunday in Ordinary Time

1 Kings 8:41-43
Galatians 1:1-2, 6-10
Luke 7:1-10

Discrimination

The virus of discrimination is still very much alive in our world today. Not only does it exist between races but also between rich and poor.

However, we do not even have to look beyond ourselves to find the discrimination virus. It's in all of us. We all have our prejudices – some from our upbringing, others from popular opinions, and still others we have acquired ourselves.

To counteract this virus of discrimination we find a solid antidote in this Sunday's readings.

In the first reading, which contains excerpts from the prayer of dedication for the new Temple in Jerusalem, King Solomon states that foreigners are to have some access to the Temple. He tells his people to respect and welcome foreigners who come to Israel because of their interest in Israel's God.

The gospel narrates an incident that happened at Capernaum. A Roman centurion who was stationed there was highly respected by the Jewish villagers. The centurion had a slave who was seriously ill. So he asked his Jewish friends to see if Jesus would cure his slave. The Jews went to Jesus, told him of how this particular centurion "loved our people" and that he had even helped them build the local synagogue.

Jesus respected the villagers' request and started off to the centurion's home. On learning of Jesus' approach, the centurion quickly sent the following message to Jesus: "I am not worthy to have you come under my roof.... But only speak the word, and let my servant be healed." Jesus was amazed at the centurion's faith and immediately cured the servant.

What a wonderful example of openness between a Roman and his Jewish friends! The two races usually hated each other. And what a reward for their friendliness!

The second reading seems to teach discrimination. For Paul curses those Jews who were teaching his Galatian converts a gospel other than the one he had taught them. These Judaizers (as they were called) insisted that all Gentile converts had to follow Jewish laws. This was wrong, Paul declared. So he curses such a perversion of the good news. In effect, the Judaizers themselves were discriminating against Paul's converts. This act of Paul was not discrimination but rather a correction of a misunderstanding.

1. Share some examples of discrimination.
2. How can we remedy forms of discrimination in our own lives and in our culture?
3. When Solomon stated that foreigners were to be allowed access to the new Temple in Jerusalem, how was he changing people's ideas on who belonged to God?
4. Reflect on Jesus' treatment of the Roman centurion and his slave. What does Jesus' action tell us?

First Sunday of Lent

Deuteronomy 26:4-10
Romans 10:8-13
Luke 4:1-13

How Soon We Forget

We've all known people born in lowly circumstances who, after climbing the social ladder, look back and snub the very community from which they had sprung.

But perhaps we, too, are guilty of this crime. Haven't we thought of ourselves as a cut above others at times? For this reason we all need to reflect on the readings for this first Sunday of Lent.

In the first reading, the author of Deuteronomy reminds his fellow Jews not to forget their lowly origins. On bringing their gifts to the Temple they are to say, "A wandering Aramean was my ancestor; he went down into Egypt and lived there as an alien...and there he became a great nation.... The Egyptians treated us harshly and afflicted us." From this oppression it was God who "with signs and wonders...brought us into this place...a land flowing with milk and honey."

The people of Israel, who came from dire poverty and fearful oppression, were thus reminded that their present good fortune was not their own doing but God's. That is why they were to offer God the first fruits of the spring harvest and "bow down before the Lord your God."

In the second reading, Paul makes it clear that all of us, no matter how lowly our origins, have been given a great future in Jesus. He says to all

Christians that, "if you confess with your lips that Jesus is Lord and believe in your heart that God raised him from the dead, you will be saved.... 'Everyone who calls on the name of the Lord shall be saved.'" Such is our good fortune. Out of spiritual poverty we rise to heavenly heights!

The gospel recounts the three temptations Jesus faced at the beginning of his public ministry. Each of the temptations encouraged Jesus to forget about his humanity. Jesus refused the bait! He did not spurn his earthly origins. Worldly kingdoms without God were nothing. Spectacular deeds without God were equally foolish.

The three readings remind us to remember our earthly origins no matter how much we are tempted to forget them. We are truly "of the earth," but we have been invited into a close participation in God's own life. Of that we cannot boast, but only be grateful.

꿈❀꿈

1. How can forgetting our roots lead us astray?
2. Reflect on the first reading. How can we today follow the example of the Jewish people, bringing gifts to the temple?
3. How does Paul, in the second reading, help the Roman Christians not to be snobbish?
4. Reflect on the gospel, particularly on how Jesus fully accepts the limits of his humanity and in so doing is an example for us to follow.

Second Sunday of Lent

Genesis 15:5-12, 17-18
Philippians 3:17–4:1
Luke 9:28b-36

God's Invitation

Robert Service, a poet of the Yukon gold rush, wrote the following lines in "The Land of Beyond":

Thank God! there is always a Land of Beyond
For us who are true to the trail;
A vision to seek, a beckoning peak,
A farness that never will fail.

The miners who went to the Yukon needed faith to search for gold despite the cold, illness, failure and innumerable other difficulties. So it must be with us Christians. Indeed, we need faith of a higher order since we seek an eternal treasure. That there is such treasure is evident from the readings for this second Sunday of Lent.

In the first reading God says to Abram, "Look toward heaven and count the stars, if you are able to count them.... So shall your descendants be." Abram believed. But how was this to happen? After all, his wife, Sarai, was barren!

To back up his promise to Abram, God commands him to prepare a covenant sacrifice. Several animals were cleft in two, thus signifying, in the custom of that time, the fate that would befall either party were they to default. Abram was duly impressed!

In the second reading Paul reminds his Philippian converts that "our citizenship is in heaven, and...the Lord Jesus Christ...will transform the body of our humiliation that it may be conformed to the body of his glory, by the power that also enables him to make all things subject to himself."

Such comforting words! The gift of faith in Christ will certainly lead us to a glorious triumph.

The gospel is that of the Transfiguration. As Jesus set his face resolutely towards Jerusalem, he was troubled. What was the purpose of his ministry? Certain death awaited him in the holy city. Was it really his Father's will that he go there?

On praying over the matter, Jesus came to a decision. It was his Father's will that he go, so go he would. At that instant the aspect of his face changed and his clothing became brilliant as lightning. Suddenly there were two men talking to him, Moses and Elijah. They spoke of his departure, which he was to accomplish in Jerusalem.

This account is Luke's way of teaching us that when we do God's will, no matter how heavy the cross, a glorious outcome is assured.

Thus for those who are true to the Christian trail there'll always be a "farness that never will fail." Though prospectors do not always find gold, we will always find eternal treasure.

$\backsim\!\circledast\!\sim$

1. When have you kept to a certain course despite great obstacles and, in the end, been rewarded?
2. How did God encourage Abram in the first reading?
3. Reflect on Paul's words of encouragement to the Philippians.
4. How does the Transfiguration encourage us in our faith journey?

Third Sunday of Lent

Exodus 3:1-8a, 13-15
1 Corinthians 10:1-6, 10-12
Luke 13:1-9

Liberating Relationships

How often we meet people who have turned away from potentially disastrous ways because of a friend or a beloved. A man with nothing to live for becomes a caregiver for a friend who is seriously ill; for her sake he gives up his wayward life. A woman who is self-centred meets a man who captures her heart; for his sake she forgets herself and becomes generous and life-giving.

These things happen all the time – sometimes dramatically, sometimes quietly. The world is filled with examples of people changing their lifestyle and their views because of love, friendship or respect for another person.

To put it another way, good relationships are liberating. But of all relationships we humans are privileged to enjoy, our relationship with God is far and away the most liberating. The readings for this Sunday bear this out.

In the first reading, God speaks to Moses from a burning bush. He is challenged by God to deliver the Hebrew people from their slavery in Egypt. Moses isn't sure he is up to such a challenge, so he questions God: "If [the Israelites] ask me, 'What is his name?' what shall I say to them?" God replied, "I AM WHO I AM." He said further, "Thus you shall say to the Israelites, 'I AM has sent me to you.'"

As we know, Moses accepted the challenge and brought about the deliverance of the Israelites. This liberating experience, called the Exodus, is still at the centre of Jewish belief. We believe it also, but for us deliverance occurs, in a final way, through Jesus leading us into a blissful eternity.

In the second reading Paul sounds a negative note. He reminds his Corinthian converts that some of their ancestors, after being liberated by Moses, nevertheless failed to please God. They broke their relationship with him, so "they were struck down in the wilderness." These things happened to our ancestors to serve as an example for us. As Paul writes, "So if you think you are standing, watch out that you do not fall."

In the gospel Jesus tells the parable of the fig tree. For three years it yielded no fruit. "Cut it down!" the master said to the tenant. But the tenant pleaded that he be allowed to "dig around it and put manure on it." If it still yielded no fruit, he would cut it down.

What the parable means is this: a living relationship with God always produces fruit. If there is no fruit, we are at fault. We've let down our side of the relationship.

Thus all three readings emphasize the deep value of a loving relationship with God. If we fail this relationship, we become imprisoned in some way. If we are faithful to our relationship with God, we are liberated – able to discover new riches and bear new fruit.

~❀~

1. Share a story where a good relationship saved someone you know and led to new life.
2. In the first reading, God's voice came to Moses from a burning bush that was not consumed. It was indeed holy ground. God then challenged Moses. Reflect on what happened. How does God challenge us today?
3. Reflect on the warning Paul gives to us in the second reading.
4. What does the gospel's parable of the fig tree mean to you?

Fourth Sunday of Lent

Joshua 5:9a, 10-12
2 Corinthians 5:17-21
Luke 15:1-3, 11-32

Homecoming

One of the happy experiences in our lives is a homecoming. After leaving our family to pursue studies, or to live on our own, we may discover that the outside world isn't as rosy as we thought. We may sorely miss the love, acceptance, warmth and nurturing we had received at home. Homecomings can bring us deep pleasure, a reassurance of our worth, a strengthening of our lives.

It is such a homecoming experience that we find in the three readings for this fourth Sunday in Lent. In the first and third readings it is explicit; in the second it is implicit.

In the first reading, Joshua leads his people back into the land of their ancestors. For 500 years they had lived in Egypt. For the next 40 they had wandered about in the Sinai desert. Now, once again, they are in the land of Abraham, Isaac and Jacob, their true home.

"Today I have rolled away from you the disgrace of Egypt," the Lord said to Joshua. "The manna ceased on the day they ate the produce of the land; ...they ate the crops of the land of Canaan that year." (Canaan later became "Israel.") At last the Israelites were once again free to raise their own crops on their own land. What is more, they were now free to worship the Lord unhindered. They were "at home."

In the second reading, Paul indicates that the real home of all peoples is in Christ. "If anyone is in Christ, there is a new creation.... In Christ, God was reconciling the world to himself, not counting their trespasses against them."

The bottom line, as Paul says, is that no one but God can forgive humanity's sin and effect a total, lasting reconciliation. God reconciled us in Christ. Only in Christ, then, are we truly "at home."

The gospel is the parable of the prodigal son or, more exactly, the merciful father. The runaway son returns home after losing everything he had, including his dignity. The father receives him with open arms and a full banquet table.

As Christians, we are called to open our arms lovingly and joyfully to all Christians who are travelling with us towards unity, and to all those who may struggle with their faith. Indeed, we are to be "home" for anyone and everyone.

All three readings for this Sunday help us to be "at home." This home is ultimately God, to whom we come through Christ and the community, the Church, which Christ promised to be with through all of time and into eternity.

1. Share an experience of homecoming.
2. How is Christ our true home?
3. As Church, we are home to all peoples. How can we best fulfill this mission?
4. What word or phrase from the readings will you carry with you this week?

Fifth Sunday of Lent

Isaiah 43:16-21
Philippians 3:8-14
John 8:1-11

The Good Old Days

How often we hear people talking fondly about "the good old days." But despite the nostalgia we have for our past, despite the laughs and the warm feelings it inspires, we all know that it's gone. We can remember it, but we cannot bring it back. Besides, deep down, we have to acknowledge that the past wasn't always all that good. In many ways we have it better now. In any case, we realize that our real challenge lies in the present and in the future. We can't change the past, but we can shape the present and the future.

This truth lies behind the readings for this fifth Sunday in Lent. They acknowledge what has gone before, but focus on the present and the future.

The first reading begins with a look back to the time of the Exodus, when God led the people out of slavery in Egypt. But right away God turns our eyes to the present and the future. "Do not remember the former things.... I am about to do a new thing." That new thing turns out to be deliverance from captivity, this time from the power of Babylon.

In the second reading Paul turns his eyes toward Christ. To the Philippians he writes: "I regard everything as loss because of the surpassing value of knowing Christ Jesus my Lord." He then goes on to say that he regards all things "as rubbish, in order that I may gain Christ." What of the future? Paul has this to say: "Forgetting what lies behind and straining forward to what lies ahead, I press on toward the goal for the prize of the heavenly call of God in Christ Jesus."

One of the great obstacles to forgetting the past and leaving it behind is sin, for sin is a dead weight. It keeps us from moving ahead. It's a failure that stands in the way of progress. It's a memory that we cannot dislodge by ourselves. This is where the gospel offers help.

Jesus meets a woman who had committed adultery. Her accusers are ready to stone her to death, in accordance with the law of Israel. Jesus knew that they, too, were sinners – more so even than the woman they were planning to kill. So he challenged anyone who was without sin to throw the first stone. No one volunteered. One by one they slunk away. Jesus then said to the woman, "Has no one condemned you?" "No one, sir," she replied. He said, "Neither do I condemn you." She was forgiven. She could face the future.

It is the same with us. When our sins are forgiven they are removed from our conscience. We are free of them, free to shape the present and prepare for the future.

1. Share some of your stories about "the good old days."
2. In the first reading God declares that he is "doing a new thing." Is God still doing "new things" today? Give some examples.
3. Reflect on how highly Paul regards Christ, as we see in the second reading.
4. Think about Jesus' forgiveness of the woman caught in adultery. How do his actions help you move past your failures and prepare for the future?

Passion Sunday

Isaiah 50:4-7
Philippians 2:6-11
Luke 22:14–23:56

Is Life Worthwhile?

In our darker moments we sometimes wonder whether life is really worth the struggle. We've experienced so many heartaches, so many failures, so many losses. The present may not be much better. Our health may be poor. Our job may have lost its appeal. Our close relationships may be at a stalemate. With such a past and such a present, the future may appear bleak indeed. Is life really worthwhile?

For help we need look no further than the readings for this Passion Sunday.

In the first reading, the prophet Isaiah speaks in the name of Israel. He recognizes that the people of Israel are God's witnesses in this world. Through Israel's many sufferings, faithfully endured, other people have a window through which to see God.

Isaiah, speaking for Israel, puts it this way: "I gave my back to those who struck me, and my cheeks to those who pulled out the beard; I did not hide my face from insult and spitting." Still, despite all these sufferings, Isaiah says, "I have set my face like flint, and I know that I shall not be put to shame."

The first Christians realized that these words of Isaiah were fulfilled perfectly in Jesus. He is the "suffering servant" par excellence. This conviction stands behind the second and third readings for this Sunday.

In the second reading, Paul teaches us that Jesus, in his humanity, was made in God's image – as were Adam and Eve. But, unlike them, he did not grasp at being God as they did. Rather, he "emptied himself, taking the form of a slave, being born in human likeness.... He humbled himself and became obedient to the point of death – even death on a cross." And because he lived out his humanity so fully, "God highly exalted him and gave him the name that is above every name."

The gospel reading is the passion narrative from Luke's gospel. In it Jesus is clearly portrayed as the suffering servant, one who made no resistance, who offered his back to those who struck him and did not turn his face against insult and spitting.

Taken together, these three readings make it abundantly clear that life is indeed worthwhile. Jesus took the worst that evil could do, yet rose from the grave glorious and immortal. Because of his sufferings all peoples are drawn to him, and through him to God.

So our sufferings, our defects, our impasses, as difficult as they may be, do not, when taken in Christian stride, keep us from fullness of life. Indeed, the opposite is true. Such sufferings fit into the glorious pattern of God's redemptive plan for all of humankind.

∽❀∾

1. Share some darker times that you have experienced in your life.
2. Reflect on Isaiah's words in the first reading depicting the sufferings of "the servant of the Lord."
3. In the second reading, Paul quotes an early Christian hymn about Jesus' self-emptying and suffering. Share your thoughts on this reading.
4. What particularly strikes you about Jesus in Luke's passion narrative?

The Triduum

The "Great Sunday"

This little book offers meditations on the Sunday Lectionary readings, and well it should, for Sunday is the original Christian feast day. From the very beginnings of the faith, Christians celebrated Eucharist on the first day of the week (as reckoned according to the Jewish calendar). Why? Sunday marked for them, as it continues to do for us, the first day of the New Creation inaugurated by Christ's resurrection from the dead. By the middle of the second century, Christians began to celebrate with special solemnity the Sunday closest to the Jewish Passover, the time of year that gives the name "paschal" to the saving mystery of Christ's death and resurrection. Quite naturally, this annual Sunday celebration at Passover time was extended to include commemorations of his last supper and his crucifixion, the dramatic events of his last days. This is the origin of the Easter Triduum, the sacred days marking "the culmination of the entire liturgical year" (*General Norms for the Liturgical Year and Calendar*, § 18).

The Easter Triduum, as its name (from Latin) indicates, comprises three days as reckoned according to ancient Jewish custom – a day was measured from sundown to sundown.

Thus, the first day of the Triduum commemorates his last supper (Holy Thursday evening) and his crucifixion, death and burial (Good Friday afternoon). There are no major liturgical celebrations on the second day (from sundown on Good Friday until sundown on Holy Saturday), for it is a period evoking the time Jesus' body rested in the tomb. The third day, the day on which Jesus rose from the dead, begins at sundown Saturday. This is the evening of the great Easter Vigil, which Saint Augustine once called the "mother of all vigils."

On these three most holy days the Church celebrates its most splendid and awe-inspiring liturgies. The Mass of the Lord's Supper on Thursday evening celebrates Jesus' last meal with his disciples when he blessed the bread and wine with the sacred words so familiar to us. This liturgy also features the ritual washing of the feet as enjoined by Jesus in John 13, and ends with the solemn procession and prayer before the reserve eucharist at a specially designated repository. The afternoon Celebration of the Lord's Passion marks the highlight of Good Friday when the Passion according to John is solemnly proclaimed, followed by special intercessory prayers for all people, the veneration of the cross, and communion. Originally celebrated from sundown on Holy Saturday evening through dawn on Easter Sunday morning, the vigil comprises the blessing of the new light and the solemn proclamation of Christ's resurrection, extensive readings from the scriptures evoking the story of salvation, the initiation of new candidates in baptism and confirmation, and culminates in the Eucharist. Easter Sunday is in essence but a continuation of this most wonderful celebration.

Anyone wishing to savour the full meaning of what each Sunday celebrates cannot miss participating in the Easter Triduum, for it is, quite simply, SUNDAY writ large.

Professor Normand Bonneau, OMI
Faculty of Theology
Saint Paul University, Ottawa

Easter Sunday

Acts 10:34a, 36-43
Colossians 3:1-4
John 20:1-18

From Darkness to Light

In the northern hemisphere, the days are shortest around December 21st; darkness prevails. But even more threatening is darkness of spirit. We all experience such times of darkness: broken relationships, sickness, financial worries, or job loss, to mention only a few. Our spirit sinks into a deep, dark sadness. But when these problems are resolved and light breaks through once again, there comes a time of peace.

The "Darkest Day Ever" was Good Friday. But the "Brightest Day Ever" was soon to follow – the first Easter Sunday. On that day, as Peter attests in the first reading, God raised Jesus. From that day onward, no darkness of the human spirit would ever be without hope. Even the darkest possible occasion, our alienation from God, was lifted in the joy of Easter, for Easter heralded God's total forgiveness.

From that Brightest Day Ever we look forward to its ultimate meaning, a meaning Paul puts so well in the second reading: "When Christ who is your life is revealed, then you also will be revealed with him in glory."

But great joy will come to us even sooner, at the time of death. For just as the risen Jesus disclosed himself to Mary Magdalen by the simple use of her name, so Jesus at our death will take us in his arms and lovingly whisper our name. We then will live on in his eternal embrace.

1. Describe a time of darkness in your life. How did light break through the darkness?
2. In your own words, explain why you recognize Easter as the greatest of feasts.
3. Many people believe in life after death. What does the Christian belief in resurrection mean to you?
4. What word or phrase from the readings will you carry with you this week?

Second Sunday of Easter

Acts 5:12-16
Revelation 1:9-11a, 12-13, 17-19
John 20:19-31

Ways Undreamed Of

We've all had the experience of having new life breathed into an enterprise that seemed to have failed. More importantly, we've also experienced new life entering into a personal relationship. Relations with a friend or a spouse may have become static or even been terminated until suddenly something happened that led to renewal and enrichment.

Keeping such experiences in mind will help us as we approach the readings for the second Sunday of the Easter season.

The followers of Jesus had been sure that the crucifixion was the end of a dream. The resurrection soon convinced them otherwise. Their dream took on new meaning, new depth. As the first reading says, "Yet more than ever believers were added to the Lord." Moreover, "people would also gather from the towns around Jerusalem, bringing the sick...and they were all cured."

Many decades later, John had a vision while exiled on the island of Patmos in Greece. As the second reading says, "I saw seven golden lampstands, and in the midst of the lampstands I saw one like the Son of Man, clothed with a long robe and with a golden sash across his chest." When John experienced this vision he fell into a dead faint. But then the figure touched him and said, "Do not be afraid; I am the first and the last, and the living one. I was dead, and see, I am alive forever and ever."

The risen Jesus is the source of all new beginnings. Where there is tragedy, even death, he can bring life. Lest any doubt remain, the gospel reading for this Sunday tells us about Thomas.

Jesus appeared to the disciples after his resurrection. "Peace be with you," he said, and he showed them his hands and his side. Then he commissioned them: "Receive the Holy Spirit. If you forgive the sins of any, they are forgiven them; if you retain the sins of any, they are retained."

But Thomas, one of the Twelve, was not present at Jesus' appearance and refused to believe. It was just too much. Eight days later Jesus came again and this time invited Thomas to touch the marks in his hands and side. Thomas replied, "My Lord and my God!" He believed. Then Jesus said, "Have you believed because you have seen me? Blessed are those who have not seen and yet have come to believe."

Whenever we think we've come to the end of the road, whenever an obstacle arises that seems insurmountable, we can remember these readings and be assured that with the risen Christ in us there are no dead ends, no impossible barriers.

1. Share your experiences of shattered dreams receiving a new life.
2. Reflect on how the resurrection of Jesus breathed new life into the discouraged disciples, as portrayed in the first reading.
3. What lessons for us do you see in the second reading, taken from the book of Revelation?
4. How does "doubting Thomas" assist us in our faith?

Third Sunday of Easter

Acts 5:27b-32, 40b-41
Revelation 5:11-14
John 21:1-19

The Planning Challenge

We are all familiar with the challenge of planning. We plan the best use of our time, we plan how best to spend our income, we plan our travels and our vacations, we plan to do this and plan to do that. Come to think of it, we devote a surprising number of hours to planning!

We are also busy fitting into plans made by others. Take politicians, for instance. They are forever proposing plans for our welfare. We are somewhat wary of them but are still interested in how we fit into them.

In the final analysis, however, we know that our personal plans, and the plans of others, do not always turn out.

Fortunately, there is one plan that will never fail. It is God's plan, the plan he has for all humanity and for the entire universe. We are challenged to take part in the unfolding of this plan. The readings for this third Sunday of Easter are concerned with this reality.

The first reading tells how the disciples of Jesus, after the resurrection, were taken before the Jewish high court for a second time. At their first trial they were given a formal command not to do any more preaching about Jesus. But they kept preaching, so they were arrested again. "You have filled Jerusalem with your teaching," the court charged, "and you are determined to bring this man's blood on us."

Peter and the disciples defended themselves, saying, "We must obey God rather than any human authority." Then they added: "The God of our ancestors raised up Jesus, whom you had killed by hanging him on a tree. God exalted him at his right hand."

God's plan was to save humanity in and through his Son. The Son fulfilled this plan despite all the plans of those who opposed him. Indeed, the very death of Jesus on the cross became central in God's unfolding plan.

In the gospel reading, Jesus "showed himself again to the disciples," this time on the shore of the Sea of Galilee. Four of his disciples had spent the night fishing but had caught nothing. As dawn broke, Jesus, from the shore, told them to cast out their net to the starboard. They obeyed him and caught so many fish they could hardly haul in the net.

The disciples' fishing plans didn't turn out until Jesus lent a hand. Then their efforts were most successful. By this miracle surely Jesus implied that henceforth they would be successful fishers of people.

In the second reading, taken from the book of Revelation, John, in a vision, saw myriad angels around the throne of God praising the Lamb that was sacrificed. All living creatures joined in this chorus of praise. John thus teaches that God's plan was unfolding successfully. This vision gives us hope. It also gives us the strength to take an ever more active part in its unfolding. We look forward with certainty to the great celebration at its completion.

1. Share some of your planning experiences – those that turned out and those that did not.
2. Reflect on how the apostles, in the first reading, acted after experiencing the risen Jesus (unlettered men facing the highest authorities in Judaism!).
3. In the second reading, John saw the Lamb being praised by all creatures in heaven and on earth. How does this vision help us as we take part in its unfolding?
4. Reflect on Peter's threefold affirmation of love in the gospel reading. How does love fit into God's unfolding plan?

Fourth Sunday of Easter

Acts 13:14, 43-52
Revelation 7:9, 14b-17
John 10:27-30

Speaking out Fearlessly

To speak out fearlessly isn't easy. But at times we must do so. We must always be diplomatic, but there are many areas in life where frank speech is a necessity. For instance, medical people have to be frank and open with patients who have a life-threatening illness.

So, too, we Christians must speak out fearlessly in matters that touch on the heart of our faith. This point is made clear in the readings for this fourth Sunday of Easter.

In the first reading, we hear of Paul and Barnabas speaking to Jewish officials. So many Jews were becoming Christian that the officials were jealous. So they blasphemed and "contradicted what was spoken by Paul." But Paul and Barnabas were undaunted. They replied, "It was necessary that the word of God should be spoken first to you. Since you reject it and judge yourselves to be unworthy of eternal life, we are now turning to the Gentiles."

And, as it turned out, the Gentiles "were glad and praised the word of the Lord." The jealous officials continued to work against the two missionaries and succeeded in having them driven out of the city. But the disciples "were filled with joy and with the Holy Spirit." Speaking out boldly for Christ paid off despite the reaction of Jewish officials in Antioch.

In the gospel reading we hear Jesus say that all those who listen to his words "will never perish. No one will snatch them out of my hand. What my Father has given me is greater than all else, and no one can snatch it out of the Father's hand." Just as Jesus spoke fearlessly, we are to listen fearlessly and, in turn, pass on Jesus' words fearlessly.

The second reading, from the book of Revelation, gives us a glimpse of the ultimate triumph awaiting those who listen to God's word and proclaim it. "After this I, John, looked, and there was a great multitude that no one could count, from every nation, from all tribes and peoples and languages, standing before the throne and before the Lamb, robed in white, with palm branches in their hands."

John was told that all these people "will hunger no more, and thirst no more." Moreover, the Lamb, "will guide them to springs of the water of life, and God will wipe away every tear from their eyes."

As Christians, our first challenge is to absorb God's word into our minds and hearts. Then we are to speak God's word fearlessly. Through us, God will lead many others to himself. Our final joy will be the greater for such courage.

1. Share an experience of speaking your mind clearly and convincingly.
2. Paul made it a practice when going into a new town to speak to the Jewish people first. Reflect together on Paul and Barnabas' experience in Antioch of Psidia (the southern part of modern Turkey).
3. When we speak out fearlessly in God's name, the gospel makes it clear that those who hear and respond will be in the Father's care. Reflect on this assurance.
4. How does the second reading from Revelation help us speak out fearlessly in God's name?

Fifth Sunday of Easter

Acts 14:21b-27
Revelation 21:1-5a
John 13:1, 31-35

The Dream of Dreams

We all have dreams about the future. Some are little, some are big. Some have to do with the near future, others have a more distant horizon. Whatever they are, we work at our dreams in order to make them reality.

Young adults, for instance, may dream of being happily married and put their efforts into bringing this about. Once they are married, they may dream of having a home of their own and so set aside part of each paycheque for that purpose. A business person dreams of success and pursues that dream by working hard and staying focused. When we've achieved our dreams we realize that there are still other dreams to be pursued. The human heart is restless. No earthly dream completely satisfies.

There is one dream, however, that does completely satisfy. Not only that – it gives heart and meaning to all our other dreams. This dream, which is the dream God has for each of us, is dropped into our lap. But once there, it makes demands of us. To learn more about this dream we turn to the readings for this fifth Sunday of the Easter season.

In the first reading we meet Paul and Barnabas as they are returning to Antioch from their first missionary journey. There they "related all that

God had done with them, and how he had opened a door of faith for the Gentiles."

Paul, Barnabas and all of us are ambassadors in carrying out God's dream, the dream of bringing all of humanity and all of creation into full union with God.

In the gospel reading Jesus, at the Last Supper, looks beyond the crucifixion and says to his followers, "Now the Son of Man has been glorified, and God has been glorified in him." In the death and resurrection of his Son, God's dream reaches a climax. That is why Jesus goes on to give a new commandment: "Just as I have loved you, you also should love one another."

This command, to love as Jesus loved, is the basic response we must give to God's presence among us. Through this response we further God's reign on earth.

The second reading tells us about the end result of God's dream: there will be "a new heaven and a new earth." There will be a holy city, a new Jerusalem "coming down out of heaven from God, prepared as a bride adorned for her husband." At that time "death will be no more; mourning and crying and pain will be no more." God's dream will have reached its eternal fulfillment.

1. Share some of the dreams you've had, or still have, for your life.
2. Reflect on the experiences of Paul and Barnabas as they ventured into new territory sharing the gospel and promoting God's dream.
3. Share your thoughts on Jesus' death/resurrection as the last act in bringing God's dream to fulfillment. Why did Jesus then give the commandment to love?
4. Try to picture the "New Jerusalem" prepared as a "bride adorned for her husband."

Sixth Sunday of Easter

Acts 15:1-2, 22-29
Revelation 21:10-14, 22-23
John 14:23-29

Courage to Change

In an earlier reflection we saw how change is an integral part of life. From the moment of birth to the hour of death we undergo change. It cannot be avoided.

By and large we take change in stride. But there are times when it is difficult – sometimes very difficult. Then we need heaps of courage. Where can we find such courage? This Sunday's readings point the way.

In the first reading, "certain individuals" (Jewish Christians) came down from Judea to Antioch and taught the Christian community there that pagan converts had to be circumcized in order to be saved. This had been the way since the time of Moses. But the New Covenant had arrived in Jesus, and in this covenant circumcision was of the heart, not of the body. To make clear this point, the church at Jerusalem sent Paul and Barnabas and others to Antioch with a strengthening message. Down through the ages, the Church has continued to come to our help when changes are in order.

In the second reading, John was given a vision of "the holy city Jerusalem coming down out of heaven from God." This "holy city Jerusalem" is a symbol of all God's people. John goes on to say, "I saw no temple in the city, for its temple is the Lord

God the Almighty and the Lamb. And the city has no need of sun or moon to shine on it, for the glory of God is its light, and its lamp is the Lamb." Surely such a vision of end-time to which we are journeying gives us the courage and strength to take changes in stride.

If we need more strength to face changes, the gospel reading comes to our aid. In it Jesus assures those who love him that "my Father will love them, and we will come to them and make our home with them." Comforting words! Then Jesus tells us, "Do not let your hearts be troubled, and do not let them be afraid."

Surely, then, we Christians of all people need have no hesitation in accepting the changes we face. God is with us through the Son and the Spirit.

✦

1. Share an experience of changing direction in your life.
2. How did the decision that circumcision was not required affect the Christian community in Paul's day?
3. How can the image of the new Jerusalem coming down from God bolster our courage?
4. How does Jesus' promise to be with us help us face change in our lives?

Ascension of the Lord

Acts 1:1-11
Hebrews 9:24-28; 10:19-23
Luke 24:46-53

Critical Junctures

During the course of life all of us come to many critical junctures. In our early years we left the security of home as we began the long process of schooling. Later on, after graduating from high school or university, we faced the challenge of earning a living in a competitive world. Then came other critical junctures, such as marriage, parenthood, a new job, or a move to a new city or country.

The first disciples faced such a critical juncture at the Ascension. Jesus had given them the truths and the example they would need. Now they were on their own to carry out the Christian challenge. But help was available.

In the first reading Luke recalls how, in his gospel, he had written about all that Jesus had taught the disciples. After his death/resurrection, Jesus had continued to teach them through forty days of appearances. Then he charged them not to leave Jerusalem but to wait for "the promise of the Father." After Jesus' ascension, two angels addressed them: "This Jesus, who has been taken up from you into heaven, will come in the same way as you saw him go into heaven."

The first disciples faced this critical juncture well, patiently waiting for the coming of the Spirit.

In the second reading, the author of Hebrews assures us that Jesus has taken away our sinfulness. We are thus new creatures, more closely related to God than ever before. Moreover, the reading ends with these comforting words: "Let us hold fast to the confession of our hope without wavering, for he who has promised is faithful."

In the gospel reading, immediately before his ascension, Jesus says: "And see, I am sending upon you what my Father promised; so stay here in the city until you have been clothed with power from on high."

Through baptism and confirmation we have been "clothed with power from on high." Hence we have the strength and courage to face all the critical junctures in our faith life as we go about witnessing to Jesus.

✌❀✎

1. Name some of the critical junctures in your everyday life or your faith life.
2. The first reading and the gospel mention the Spirit that is given to us. How does the Spirit work in our lives?
3. Share your thoughts on holding fast to what the second reading describes as the "confession of our hope without wavering."
4. What word or phrase from the readings will you carry with you this week?

Pentecost

Acts 2:1-11
Romans 8:8-17
John 14:15-16, 23b-26

The Times Are a-Changing

They certainly are! And at an ever-increasing pace. How should we respond? If the changes promote human welfare, we should do our best to support them. If they diminish human welfare, we should do our best to thwart them. As Christians we have an agenda of our own for change. Indeed, we are challenged to change the world!

The feast of Pentecost is about precisely such a challenge. The first reading sets the tone of the challenge, assuring us that as we work at changing the world the Holy Spirit is with us. Tongues as of fire rested on each of the apostles and "all of them were filled with the Holy Spirit and began to speak in other languages, as the Spirit gave them ability."

In the second reading Paul makes it clear that all Christians are gifted with the Spirit. "But you are not in the flesh; you are in the Spirit, since the Spirit of God dwells in you." Thus the same Spirit that came upon the apostles also comes to all Christians.

In the gospel reading Jesus assures his followers that he will give them "another Advocate, to be with you forever." This Spirit, Jesus promises, "will teach you everything, and remind you of all that I have said to you."

Wow! What a fire at Pentecost! It's still burning, changing our world into a new heaven and a new earth. And we, the Spirit's envoys, are challenged to keep the Pentecost fire burning so all peoples will be able to cry out, as we do, "Abba, Father!"

1. How do you see our world as a fast-changing one?
2. Reflect on what happened at the first Pentecost.
3. How does the Spirit "teach us everything," as the gospel says?
4. How can you help others cry out, "Abba, Father!"?

Trinity Sunday

Proverbs 8:22-31
Romans 5:1-5
John 16:12-15

Sources of Courage

The readings of last Sunday, the feast of Pentecost, helped us realize our part in shaping the fast-moving world of today. Lest we find this task too difficult, the readings for this Sunday, the feast of the Trinity, bolster our courage.

The first reading, from Proverbs, assures us that the wisdom of God was at work from the very beginning of creation. As the reading says, "Ages ago I was set up, at the first, before the beginning of the earth." Furthermore, wisdom, from the beginning, was "rejoicing in his inhabited world and delighting in the human race." Now that's comforting! Today, as never before, we are discovering more and more about the secrets of the universe, and about ourselves (in whom wisdom finds delight).

The second reading, from Paul to the Romans, assures us that through Christ "we have peace with God" and so we can "boast in our hope of sharing the glory of God." All this "because God's love has been poured into our hearts through the Holy Spirit that has been given to us."

In the gospel, Jesus tells his followers that they are not yet ready to hear all the truths he would love to share with them, but he continues, "When the Spirit of truth comes, he will guide you into all the truth." This same Spirit,

Jesus concludes, "will take what is mine and declare it to you."

We can thus go about the challenge of doing our part in giving final shape to the world. For with us and in us is the Father Creator, the Son Redeemer, and the Spirit Enlivener. What greater sources of courage could there be?

～❀～

1. What are the challenges of shaping the world?
2. Reflect on how wisdom rejoiced in the inhabited world and delighted in the human race (see the first reading).
3. Paul assured the Romans that "we boast in our hope of sharing the glory of God." What does this mean to you?
4. How does the Spirit enable each age to face and solve new problems and put old truths in new clothing?

Body and Blood of Christ

Genesis 14:18-20
1 Corinthians 11:23-26
Luke 9:11b-17

Symbols

"It's only a symbol," I hear people say. I find their comment sad, for symbols are meant to be real – very real. Indeed, they are an integral part of our humanity.

Take a wedding ring, for instance. A wedding ring is much more than a piece of jewellery. It touches on a deep reality – a spousal relationship – by recalling and deepening it.

This understanding of symbols will help us better appreciate the feast of Christ's Body and Blood and deepen our understanding of the readings (words, too, are symbols).

The first reading tells of Abram's victory over the abductors of his nephew Lot. To celebrate this victory Melchizedek, king of Jerusalem, "brought out bread and wine" and proceeded to bless Abram. The meal and blessing (both symbols) deepened the appreciation of Abram's victory.

In the gospel, Luke recalls the miracle of the multiplication of loaves and fish in eucharistic language. Jesus took up "the five loaves and the two fish, he looked up to heaven, and blessed and broke them, and gave them to the disciples to set before the crowd."

In the second reading, Paul passes on to his Corinthian converts the foundations of the Eucharist that he himself had "received from the

Lord." During the Last Supper, Jesus "took a loaf of bread, and when he had given thanks, he broke it and said, 'This is my body that is for you. Do this in remembrance of me.' In the same way he took the cup also, after supper, saying, 'This cup is the new covenant in my blood. Do this, as often as you drink it, in remembrance of me.'"

Through and in the symbols of the readings, the eating and drinking of the eucharistic bread and wine, the gathered community and the presider, the risen Jesus comes to us, freeing us from evil and opening us up to a fuller participation in God's reign.

1. How do symbols (hugs, handshakes, words, colours, art, etc.) operate in our society?
2. Reflect on the gospel reading. How does it connect with the Eucharist?
3. Reread the final paragraph of this reflection. What does it mean to you?
4. What word or phrase from the readings will you carry with you this week?

Tenth Sunday in Ordinary Time

1 Kings 17:8-9, 17-21a, 22-24
Galatians 1:11-19
Luke 7:11-17

In the Throes of Helplessness

We see and read and hear about people who seem totally helpless – poor people in developing countries, the incurably sick, those imprisoned for life, and others who live in dire situations.

And what about us? Do we not also experience times of helplessness? Indeed we do. Many's the time we do not know which way to turn. So we all need deliverance. We all need healing. We all need assurance and courage. But where can we find these things? Our heart tells us that such help must be available somewhere, for without it life would only lead to despair. Fortunately, this is more than just a feeling. We have the assurance of God's help. That assurance comes out loud and clear in the readings for this tenth Sunday in Ordinary Time.

The first reading tells us about a widow who had just lost her only son, the sole means of her future support. The prophet Elijah, to whom she had given help, comes to her aid. Elijah prayed to God, "'O Lord my God, let this child's life come into him again.' The Lord listened to the voice of Elijah…and [the child] revived."

Clearly, Israel's God (and our God) is a compassionate God.

In the second reading, Paul tells the Galatians that God had called him and revealed his Son to him in order that he would proclaim the Son to the Gentiles. The Gentiles of Paul's day, and the "strangers" of our own day, stand helpless and often hopeless in the face of life's tragedies.

In the gospel, we are told how Jesus meets up with a funeral procession in the town of Nain. The only son of a widow was being buried. Jesus "had compassion for her." Approaching the stretcher he said, "Young man, I say to you, rise! The dead man sat up and began to speak, and Jesus gave him to his mother."

These three readings thus emphasize that God is a God of compassion. They also clearly indicate that as God's people we are to be compassionate towards others. We are to minister – to heal, forgive, enlighten, encourage and assure – to those who are afflicted and helpless.

1. Have you ever been in great need and had someone come to your aid? Share your story or that of someone you know.
2. Some people grew up in an era where God was looked upon as a God of judgment. How does Elijah's story in the first reading correct that image?
3. Like the widow in Elijah's story, the widow of Nain lost her only son. Compare the two cures.
4. How does our Christian faith help us when we feel helpless?

Eleventh Sunday in Ordinary Time

2 Samuel 12:7-10, 13
Galatians 2:16, 19-21
Luke 7:36–8:3

Healing

How relieved we are when someone whom we have hurt forgives us, especially when that someone is close to our heart. Such forgiveness comes to us like a soft, refreshing breeze. A load is lifted. It heals our hurt. We feel whole again.

If this is our reaction to human forgiveness, how do we respond to God's forgiveness? God's healing forgiveness is the theme of this Sunday's readings.

In the first reading, the prophet Nathan confronts David with his sins of adultery and murder – adultery with Bathsheba and the subsequent killing of her husband, Uriah. David accepts Nathan's rebuke and acknowledges, "I have sinned against the Lord." Nathan replies, "Now the Lord has put away your sin; you shall not die."

David's failure was most serious. Yet, when he repented, God was quick to forgive. Not only did God forgive David, God did not in any way take back the promises he had made to David and his descendants.

In the second reading, Paul makes the following point: "We know that a person is justified not by the works of the law but through faith in Jesus Christ." This was a crucial point for Paul. Up to the time of Christ, the faithful were justified through obedience to the law.

This was no longer the case. Justification now comes through faith in Christ. Paul put it this way: "And the life I now live in the flesh I live by faith in the Son of God, who loved me and gave himself for me." Forgiveness thus comes to us as pure gift.

The gospel is wonderfully shocking! In story form it exemplifies the healing compassion Jesus has for sinners. A Pharisee invited Jesus to eat with him. During the meal a woman whom all knew to be a sinner burst into the gathering and "weeping...began to bathe his feet with her tears." Horrors! No respectable woman would ever have done that! But the sinful woman did. Jesus was there and that was all that mattered to her. She was totally taken with his great compassion.

What a picture! The Pharisees were embarrassed by her presence. Moreover, they thought themselves superior to Jesus, who seemed oblivious of the woman's sinfulness. Seeing her sorrow Jesus said, "Your sins are forgiven.... Your faith has saved you; go in peace."

⌒✾⌒

1. Share an experience of forgiving others or of being forgiven.
2. Reflect on David's sin and his forgiveness by God.
3. Paul emphasizes that we are forgiven not by following the law but by faith in Christ. What does this mean to you?
4. Reflect on the gospel reading. With whom do you identify in this story? Why?

Twelfth Sunday in Ordinary Time

Zechariah 12:10-11
Galatians 3:26-29
Luke 9:18-24

Ups and Downs

One of Shakespeare's sayings goes like this: "The course of true love never did run smooth." Lovers know the truth of these words. One day they may be on top of the world and the next day, down in the dumps.

Lovers have such ups and downs simply because love is relational. It has to do with two people striving to know one another and at the same time grow together. Because of human weakness this challenge is anything but easy, so ups and downs on the path of love are inevitable. But both are good and necessary. Without "ups" lovers would lose courage; without "downs" their true characters would not surface.

Spiritual life is no different, for all of us are journeying in love towards God. Because of our weakness, this journey is by no means smooth. It, too, has its ups and downs, as we see when we reflect on the readings for this Sunday.

In the first reading the prophet Zechariah, writing after the Babylonian exile, says in God's name, "I will pour out a spirit of compassion and supplication on the house of David and the inhabitants of Jerusalem." To these joyful words Zechariah adds this sombre note: "When they look on the one whom they have pierced, they shall mourn for him."

The second reading reminds us that we Christians are "baptized into Christ" and "have clothed [ourselves] with Christ." Hence we are to live as Christ lived. This takes us to the gospel, which considers Jesus' identity.

Jesus asks his disciples, "Who do the crowds say that I am?" After receiving various answers, including Peter's, Jesus makes clear that as Messiah, he "must undergo great suffering, and be rejected by the elders, chief priests, and scribes, and be killed, and on the third day be raised." Then Jesus also made it clear that his followers were to take up their cross daily and follow him.

Thus the "ups" of our spiritual lives are that we are clothed with Christ and so are heirs to the promises of an eternal life of happiness. Our "downs" are when sufferings (the cross) come our way – but even such sufferings are lessened when we take them as a sharing in the life of Christ.

~※~

1. Share some of the ups and downs you may have experienced in the process of becoming close friends with someone.
2. In the second reading, how does Paul help us realize the joys of being Christians?
3. Reflect on why Jesus accepted suffering and death to bring us new life.
4. How do we share in the cross of Christ?

Thirteenth Sunday in Ordinary Time

1 Kings 19:16b, 19-21
Galatians 5:1, 13-18
Luke 9:51-62

Enthusiasm

Think back to a time when you were beginning an enterprise with great gusto and high enthusiasm. You worked at it wholeheartedly. Gradually, your interest lessened. You spent less time on it. Eventually you dropped out of it.

This is a common human experience. But, fortunately, there is a sequel. If the enterprise was truly worthwhile we can regain our enthusiasm for it. We can take it up again at an even deeper level and with a wiser frame of mind.

As Christians we have entered into the greatest enterprise the world has known, thanks to God's grace. If our enthusiasm has waned, even if it has disappeared, it can be regained. The flame can be rekindled. This is one of the lessons contained in the readings for this Sunday.

In the first reading Elijah, who is now elderly, wishes to pass on his prophetic call to Elisha. But Elisha first wants to say goodbye to his parents. Elijah wonders whether Elisha will return. Not only does he return, he slaughters the oxen and offers them in sacrifice, indicating his complete acceptance of the prophetic task.

A similar incident takes place in the gospel reading. Jesus invites a listener to "follow me." But the listener replies, "Lord, first let me go and bury my father." Jesus says, "Let the dead bury their own dead; but as for you, go and proclaim the kingdom of God." The point he is making is that the proclamation of the kingdom is "the" great enterprise. Its demands take precedence over everything else. In this shocking way Jesus emphasizes the centrality of God's kingdom and the role we are to play in it.

The second reading makes clear what the kingdom of God is all about: "For freedom Christ has set us free." That's good news indeed! We are slaves to narrow horizons. Only in Christ can we be truly free. Only in Christ can we regain our enthusiasm for the kingdom of God.

1. Share an experience of losing enthusiasm and later regaining it.
2. The first reading and the gospel point to the importance of doing God's work. What does this mean to you?
3. Reflect on how Jesus frees us.
4. What word or phrase from the readings will you carry with you this week?

Fourteenth Sunday in Ordinary Time

Isaiah 66:10-14c
Galatians 6:14-18
Luke 10:1-12, 17-20

Shalom

Culture, not the dictionary, gives meaning to words. For words acquire their meaning from accepted usage, and usage is largely determined by the culture we live in.

Culture ultimately derives from what people believe about human life. These beliefs give content to the words we use.

For instance, take the word "peace." Were you to ask people in the Western world what peace means, you would probably be told something like this: "It's the absence of wars and having friendly relationships with people." That is true, as far as it goes, but in the Judeo-Christian tradition, peace has a deeper meaning.

We Christians trace the word "peace" to the Jewish word *shalom*. To the Jews, *shalom* means being one with God, their family and their neighbour, as well as oneness within the heart and oneness with the created world. Moreover, this oneness, this *shalom*, is seen not as a human accomplishment but as a gift from God.

With this insight in mind, we take up the readings for this Sunday.

In the first reading we hear Isaiah proclaim, "For thus says the Lord: 'I will extend prosperity to [Jerusalem] like a river.'" After fifty years in the Babylonian exile, the Jewish people are once again in their own city, Jerusalem. Now they have *shalom* – peace. God's presence is fully with them. Isaiah, speaking in God's name, says, "As a mother comforts her child, so I will comfort you."

In the second reading Paul makes it clear that for Christians, the true basis for peace is "the cross of our Lord Jesus Christ." For those who accept the cross, Paul says, "Peace be upon them, and mercy, and upon the Israel of God."

In the gospel Luke relates how Jesus sent out 72 disciples to visit homes and say, "Peace to this house!" They were then to cure the sick and declare, "The kingdom of God has come near to you." For only in and through the reign of God can there be true peace.

As we share the greeting of peace at the Eucharist each week we would do well to remember the true depth of Christian peace. Ultimately, peace is a participation in the reign of God – now partially, but in heaven, fully. *Shalom*!

1. Share some of the popular understandings of "peace."
2. How did the Jewish people associate peace with Jerusalem?
3. Reflect on the connection between the cross and peace.
4. What is the connection between peace and the kingdom of God?

Fifteenth Sunday in Ordinary Time

Deuteronomy 30:10-14
Colossians 1:15-20
Luke 10:25-37

A Fragmented Society

In today's world, despite the fact that we are fast becoming a global village, we are still suspicious about our differences. We do not understand enough about each other's cultures, each other's religions. To some extent, we remain a fragmented society.

What can bring us together? Surely one answer has something to do with our common humanity. And where better to discover what it means to be human than from our creator's own words? This Sunday's readings touch closely on this very point.

The first reading, from the book of Deuteronomy, makes clear that we are all creatures of God, and that God has given us the Ten Commandments, commandments that point to what we are as human beings. Only in keeping these commands, this covenant with God, can we be truly human. For all the commandments are deeply rooted in the human heart.

In the second reading, Paul points out that Christ is "the firstborn of all creation" and that "all things have been created through him and for him." Moreover, he adds that in Christ "God was pleased to reconcile to himself all things …through the blood of his cross."

In Christ, and only in him, can we be fully human and at peace with all creation.

The gospel is the parable of the good Samaritan. To catch its full meaning, remember that in the time of Jesus, "neighbour" to the Jewish people meant another Jew. Gentiles were not "neighbours." So Jesus, in answer to the lawyer's question, told the story of the badly beaten man who was neglected by a Jewish priest and a Jewish Levite but helped by a hated Samaritan.

Jesus came to fulfill the covenant. Part of this fulfillment was to redefine who belonged to God's people. Hitherto it was circumcision, plus the keeping of the law, that defined the people of God. In the parable of the good Samaritan, however, Jesus makes clear that God's people are those who show compassion towards others.

Were all people to take this parable to heart, our world would cease to be fragmented. Instead, we would be more compassionate to one another, more understanding, more united.

1. Share some directions that would help us live without being suspicious of differences.
2. How does keeping the Ten Commandments bring us together?
3. What vision of life does Paul give us in the second reading?
4. Share your insights on the parable of the good Samaritan.

Sixteenth Sunday in Ordinary Time

Genesis 18:1-10a
Colossians 1:24-28
Luke 10:38-42

A Question of Priority

In our busy, fast-moving world, we simply must set priorities. There are too many directions to take, too many tasks to fulfill, too many voices to heed, too many factors to take into account. Without setting our priorities we'd be like a boat caught in a huge whirlpool, spinning around and getting nowhere.

The readings for this Sunday back up this contention.

In the first reading, Abraham, in the heat of the day, sees three men standing before him. Instead of asking their names, where they come from, or where they are going, he immediately looks after their physical needs. In desert country, such needs were a priority. In recompense for his hospitality one of the three made Abraham a promise: "Your wife Sarah shall have a son." Good news indeed, for Abraham and Sarah had given up hope of having an heir.

In the second reading, Paul assures the Colossians that he rejoices "in my sufferings for your sake." In doing so he is "completing what is lacking in Christ's afflictions for the sake of his body, that is, the church." Paul sees his suffering for others as a top priority.

The gospel describes Jesus' visit to a village where "Martha welcomed him into her home."

But then Martha became distracted in the face of the many things that needed to be done, whereas her sister, Mary, "sat at the Lord's feet and listened to what he was saying." Mary had her priorities straight – the life-giving words of Jesus come first. For this, Jesus commended her.

1. Share an experience of setting priorities. How did you know what was most important?
2. Reflect on Abraham's priorities and the reward he received.
3. Why does Paul put priority on his suffering? What does he mean when he says, "Christ in you, the hope of glory"?
4. In the gospel, why was Mary's choice better than Martha's? Was Jesus really criticizing Martha's actions?

Seventeenth Sunday in Ordinary Time

Genesis 18:20-21, 23-32
Colossians 2:6-14
Luke 11:1-13

Learning to Pray

How marvellous is the gift of learning! From childhood on, the many marvels of the vast created world open up to us. Through our parents and teachers, through our reading and experience, we come to know the world of nature and stories of human struggles and achievements.

From our earliest years, most of us also learn about God. We've learned about creation and redemption. But we still, perhaps, are not able to talk openly and familiarly with God. Thus we all need to heed the readings of this Sunday, which have much to tell us about prayer.

In the first reading we learn how generous God is to those in need. The people of Sodom and Gomorrah committed serious sins. As a result, it seemed that God was about to destroy them. But Abraham pleaded for them (for he was to be the father "of all nations"). He asked God to spare them if 50 just people could be found there. God agreed. But Abraham pushed a little further. Would God spare them if 45 just people could be found? God agreed again. Finally, would God spare the cities if only ten just ones could be found? And God generously agreed.

The second reading also encourages us to go to God in our need, for in baptism we were "buried with Christ," and being close to Christ we are close to God.

In the gospel, one of the disciples asks Jesus, in the name of all of us, "Lord, teach us to pray." And teach us Jesus did. He taught us the "Our Father," a prayer that, as St. Augustine said, contains the seeds of all our needs.

1. Why do we need others?
2. What can we learn from Abraham about prayer in the first reading?
3. As Paul attests in the second reading, we "have received Christ Jesus the Lord." How might this truth affect our prayer life?
4. Though Luke's "Our Father" is shorter than Matthew's, it still teaches us the true heart of prayer. How do you see the various parts of the Our Father as Luke recounts them?

Eighteenth Sunday in Ordinary Time

Ecclesiastes 1:2; 2:21-23
Colossians 3:1-5, 9-11
Luke 12:13-21

Tinsel Chasing

The above title is not the name of a new game! In fact, it's the name of a very old one – it goes back to the days of Adam and Eve. The game I refer to is that of pursuing the goods of this world in the belief that they will entirely satisfy our longings. The sad news is that all of us, in one way or another, are caught up in this game. What can we do to free ourselves?

A remedy lies close at hand – indeed, as close as this Sunday's readings.

The first reading begins with these oft-quoted words from the book of Ecclesiastes: "Vanity of vanities! All is vanity." These words are followed by a question: "What do people gain from all the toil at which they toil under the sun?"

How wise are these inspired words! After acquiring this or that gain, this or that pleasure, we always look for something more. Having found the something more, our yearning does not cease. We keep on looking, even though nothing in this world will ever completely satisfy us.

In the second reading, Paul tells his Colossian converts to "seek the things that are above, where Christ is, seated at the right hand of God." The reading ends with the claim that "Christ is all and in all!"

The gospel begins with two brothers asking Jesus to settle their property claims. Jesus refuses to do so. Then he says to them, and to everyone of us, "Take care! Be on your guard against all kinds of greed; for one's life does not consist in the abundance of possessions."

For Christians, and indeed for all peoples, an emphasis on tinsel is out. Our hearts need much more to satisfy them. This satisfaction can be found only in and through Christ.

⌒☸⌒

1. Describe a time of "tinsel chasing" in your own life.
2. What does the author of Ecclesiastes mean by the words "Vanity of vanities! All is vanity"?
3. When Paul tells us in the second reading to set our minds on the things that are above, does he mean we are to have no interest in worldly pursuits?
4. Share your thoughts on the gospel for this Sunday, especially on Jesus' refusal to settle land claims and on the parable of the farmer who built larger barns.

Nineteenth Sunday in Ordinary Time

Wisdom 18:6-9
Hebrews 11:1-2, 8-19
Luke 12:32-48

Encouraging Words

From our earliest years, people around us have encouraged us. When we attempted our first steps, Mom and Dad, and perhaps older brothers and sisters, were there with open arms urging us to trust them. At school we were offered various rewards if we did well. Even as adults we hesitate in the face of new challenges. To accept them we often need to be encouraged.

In our spiritual lives, too, we need encouragement. This truth is exemplified in the readings for this Sunday.

In the first reading, we hear about the Jewish people languishing in Egyptian slavery. To escape from slavery, they needed some assurance of success. Encouragement was given to them in the form of the severe plagues visited upon the Egyptians. These plagues bolstered the Israelites' courage, and they joined in the "exodus."

The second reading describes how God encouraged Abraham to leave his land by promising that Abraham would have many descendants – "as many as the stars of heaven and as the innumerable grains of sand by the seashore." This promise strengthened Abraham's determination to seek out a new home.

In the gospel reading, Jesus encourages his followers, saying, "Do not be afraid, little flock, for it is your Father's good pleasure to give you the kingdom." He continues, "Be dressed for action and have your lamps lit." God's reign, now begun, invites us into the future.

God is faithful to his promises. When God invites us to take up the challenge, we must not hesitate to accept.

∽❀∼

1. Describe a time when someone encouraged you to embrace a new challenge.
2. In the background of the first reading, God chose Moses to lead the people out of slavery and gave him power to work many wonders in order to encourage them. What effect did these wonders have on the Israelites?
3. Why did Abraham leave home to journey into an unknown land? Reflect on the promise God made to him, a promise that touches all of us.
4. How, in the gospel, does God encourage us in our faith journey through the promise of the "kingdom"?

Twentieth Sunday in Ordinary Time

Jeremiah 38:1-2, 4-6, 8-10
Hebrews 12:1-4
Luke 12:49-53

Bad News / Good News

When relatives, friends or neighbours meet there is often a sharing of bad news and good news. Life's like that. So, too, are our sacred Scriptures. They mirror human life, giving it a new and greater depth.

This Sunday's readings exemplify the above truth. Each of the readings contains both bad news and good news.

In the first reading, the prophet Jeremiah begins with bad news. Jerusalem was under siege by a foreign army. Jeremiah prophesied that Jerusalem would fall. Soldiers and citizens did not like this prophecy; as a result, Jeremiah was thrust into a deep pit and left to die. Bad news! But he was rescued. Good news!

In the second reading, the author of the letter to the Hebrews tells how Jesus "endured the cross, disregarding its shame, and has taken his seat at the right hand of the throne of God." Jesus gave up his life that we might live. Bad news quickly became good news.

In the gospel, Jesus continues the bad news/good news theme found in the two previous readings. He says, "I have a baptism with which to be baptized, and what stress I am under until it is completed!" As it happened, the great stress of the cross gave way to the inestimable joy of resurrection.

On balance, in our own lives and in the life of the world, the good news towers over the bad. The last word for human history and for our universe is Glory.

1. Share some experiences of the bad news/ good news aspect of life.
2. In what way does Jeremiah's plight in the first reading remind us of Jesus' cross/resurrection?
3. How did the cross of Jesus become good news? What does this mean for us?
4. Jesus came, as the gospel makes clear, "to bring fire to the earth" as well as to bring about "division." Reflect on this good news/ bad news.

Twenty-first Sunday in Ordinary Time

Isaiah 66:18-21
Hebrews 12:5-7, 11-13
Luke 13:22-30

God Can't Be Boxed In

We humans have a tendency to swing material possessions, and even other people, into our own small orbits. Possessions and people, at least some people, belong to us (or so we think), as if they are here to serve our own limited purposes. Few people openly claim to do this, but some of our actions say otherwise.

The people who implicitly believe that life centres on them will even include the Divine as part of their world. But God refuses to be boxed in: for God is the God of all creation, and, as such, centres all reality. This truth clearly emerges in the readings for this Sunday.

People in the Old Testament tended to regard God as their own possession. But God refused to be owned. Through the prophet Isaiah, in the first reading, God declares, "I am coming to gather all nations and tongues; and they shall come and shall see my glory."

In the gospel Jesus is asked, "Lord, will only a few be saved?" Jesus refuses to give a direct answer. Rather, he goes right to the heart of the salvation process, saying, "Strive to enter through the narrow door." In other words, those who will be saved are those who are faithful to God's word, especially to the "word" that "became flesh." Jesus is indeed the door to eternal life.

Lest we swing the world around our own little selves, God disciplines us, trains us, forms us. As the second reading teaches, "The Lord disciplines those whom he loves, and chastises every child whom he accepts."

God's discipline helps us break out of our own enclosed world and brings us to the realization that it is God who centres the universe.

1. In what ways do we tend to centre the world around ourselves?
2. How do we box God in (perhaps without realizing it)?
3. Share some examples of the way God disciplines us.
4. What word or phrase from the readings will you carry with you this week?

Twenty-second Sunday
in Ordinary Time

Sirach 3:17-20, 28-29
Hebrews 12:18-19, 22-24a
Luke 14:1, 7-14

An Upside-down Guest List

Get-togethers often involve extended family or common-interest groups. Such gatherings are good. We need them to feel connected. But other get-togethers are more exclusive, and often snobbish. Those invited are of the so-called elite.

This latter type of gathering is the object of this Sunday's readings. For even in ancient times groups with selfish agendas were in existence.

The first reading, from the book of Sirach, contains a lesson in humility. The author cautions us, "Perform your tasks with humility." We are to seek the Lord's "favour," not popular acclaim. To the truly humble, the author assures us, "the Lord reveals his secrets."

In the second reading, the author of Hebrews reminds Christians that all Christian gatherings are pointed towards "the heavenly Jerusalem," where the faithful will gather around Jesus and rejoice in a close, common unity.

In the gospel, Jesus comes out swinging! "Do not sit down at the place of honour" when you attend banquets, he says. And he continues: "When you give a luncheon or a dinner, do not invite your friends or your brothers or sisters or your relatives or rich neighbours." Wow! Straight from the shoulder! Does this statement upset us?

It should. It is a powerful reminder that the poor, the defenceless, the weak are truly our neighbours and should never be neglected.

Such an "upside-down guest list" is a powerful antidote to the selfishness and exclusivity of "in" groups.

～❀～

1. Share your thoughts on the lessons of humility found in the first reading.
2. What does humility have to do with groups?
3. Ponder the two great lessons Jesus teaches us about group gatherings.
4. What word or phrase from the readings will you carry with you this week?

Twenty-third Sunday in Ordinary Time

Wisdom 9:13-18
Philemon 9b-10, 12-17
Luke 14:25-33

Jesus' Advice on "How-to"

In this practical age of ours, there are "how-to" books on almost any skill you wish to acquire. There are "how-to" books on computers, plumbing, sewing, investing, sports, and much more. Name your interest and you'll find a book on how to pursue it.

There are also "how-to"s in our Christian life. They engage us on a much deeper level than do the worldly ones, however. What Jesus gave us are guidelines. The central guideline he gave is "Follow me." As Paul says, we are to put on the mind and heart of Jesus. Only in so doing can we make the many on-the-spot decisions we face each day; the risen Jesus gives us the wisdom and strength.

The three scripture readings for this Sunday exemplify the guidelines for our Christian lives.

The first reading, from the book of Wisdom, stands as a preface to the other two readings. It makes the point that there is only one source of true wisdom: God. As the reading says, "the reasoning of mortals is worthless, and our designs are likely to fail.... We can hardly guess at what is on earth...but who has traced out what is in the heavens?"

Fortunately, God has given us an insight into his own wisdom. As the author of the book of

Wisdom writes, "Who has learned your counsel, unless you have given wisdom and sent your holy spirit from on high?" Thus, we humans have been "taught what pleases [God], and were saved by wisdom."

This wisdom, God's gift to us, is made concrete in the second reading and in the gospel.

In the second reading, Paul, while in prison in Rome, writes to Philemon, a convert of his living in Greece. He tells Philemon that he has met and converted Philemon's runaway slave, Onesimus. He is sending Onesimus back, but asks Philemon to treat him not just as a slave but as a brother in Christ.

In other words, the wisdom of God challenges us to treat all human beings as brothers and sisters. True religion is not abstract or apart from daily life. True religion is down-to-earth, practical love for our neighbour.

The gospel balances the lesson of the second reading. We must love one another, yes, but we cannot do so fully unless we put Jesus first in our lives. Jesus says, "Whoever comes to me and does not hate father and mother, spouse and children, brothers and sisters, yes, and even life itself, cannot be my disciple. Whoever does not carry the cross and follow me cannot be my disciple."

To us, these are extremely harsh words! We wouldn't use them. But at the time of Jesus they were the way of saying that there can be only one supreme love in anyone's life. All other loves are to be secondary – that is, all things that stand in the way of this love are to be "hated."

Jesus concludes the gospel with these words: "None of you can become my disciple if you do not give up all your possessions." That is, our hearts are to be wholly given to Jesus so that our heartstrings are not attached to worldly goods.

The three readings for this Sunday do indeed give us solid "how-to"s for living our Christian lives.

～❀～

1. Describe a time in your life where worldly wisdom fell short and divine wisdom offered the best guidance.
2. Recall an experience you've had where money or power came first and people came second.
3. Think of a time in your life when love of God and love for self or neighbour clashed. How did the situation resolve itself?
4. What can you do to bring more of God's wisdom into your life?

Twenty-fourth Sunday
in Ordinary Time

Exodus 32:7-11, 13-14
1 Timothy 1:12-17
Luke 15:1-32

At the Negotiating Table

In this age of union–management conflict, we have become familiar with the word "mediator." Mediators are often called on to settle disputes over wages and working conditions.

We are also familiar with a third party's role in bringing about a reconciliation between two individuals.

But do we give any thought to mediators between us and God? This Sunday's readings have to do with this question.

The first reading tells us how the chosen people rebelled shortly after their deliverance from Egypt. Moses, their leader, climbed Mount Sinai to commune with God. In his absence, the people "cast for themselves an image of a calf, and...worshipped it."

In anger, God said to Moses: "Now let me alone, so that my wrath may burn hot against them and I may consume them; and of you I will make a great nation."

But Moses pleaded, "Remember Abraham, Isaac and Israel." So "the Lord changed his mind about the disaster that he planned to bring on his people." Moses was a successful mediator.

But humanity's conflict with God was not over. A deeper healing was necessary. The next two readings tell us about the mediator who brought about this healing.

Paul persecuted the followers of Christ. Later, he says, "I received mercy because I had acted ignorantly in unbelief." Based on his experience of forgiveness, he makes this solemn declaration: "The saying is sure and worthy of full acceptance, that Christ Jesus came into the world to save sinners."

The gospel relates two familiar parables: the shepherd who had a flock of 100 sheep and left the 99 to seek the one that was lost, and the woman who had ten silver coins, lost one, and searched diligently until she found it.

These parables powerfully highlight Jesus' role as mediator. In real life, few shepherds would leave 99 sheep to search for one that was lost. And few people would be concerned enough to search until they found one lost coin.

But Jesus is different. So much does he love each of us, so precious are we to him, that when we turn our back on God, Jesus will not rest until we are reconciled.

What a great comfort this is! For who among us has not strayed at times from our shepherd? And who has not been lost at times in the obscuring whirlwinds of life? Be assured that Jesus, the incomparable mediator, will seek us out. He will help us to be reconciled and be rejoined to the flock.

1. Have you ever acted as a mediator or been helped by a mediator? Describe your experience.
2. Name some qualities of a good mediator. How do these apply to Jesus?
3. Describe a time when you felt great appreciation for Jesus the mediator.
4. What steps can you take to let Jesus be a mediator in your life?

Twenty-fifth Sunday in Ordinary Time

Amos 8:4-7
1 Timothy 2:1-7
Luke 16:1-13

No Place for the Ruthless in a "People" Kingdom

Ordinary, good-living people are "people people." In their day-to-day living, they rate people over material gain.

There are others, however, to whom material gain comes first. In the glitter of gain, all else fades into insignificance, even people. These are the fortune-seekers of this world. To them, money is an idol to be worshipped, and people are pawns.

In the first reading for this Sunday, the prophet Amos has harsh words for such cold-hearted fortune-seekers: "Hear this, you that trample on the needy, and bring to ruin the poor of the land." Amos knew that they wished the Sabbath were over quickly so that they might resume their swindling practices.

In the gospel, Jesus uses a parable to praise an enterprising manager for his financial astuteness.

The manager handled his master's business so badly that the master had no choice but to dismiss him. He had no other skills or ways of making a living. He was really in a tight corner.

Suddenly, he had an idea. Why not reduce the debts of the people who owed his master?

In this way, the master would get some of what he was owed. The debtors, whose debt was reduced, would be favourably disposed towards the manager.

For this astute decision, the master praised him. Under the circumstances, it was a wise approach.

Jesus then concludes the parable, saying, "And I tell you, make friends for yourselves by means of dishonest wealth so that when it is gone, they may welcome you into the eternal homes."

Money is thus for people, not people for money. And there's more: When money is used for people, God is pleased and so it becomes a preparation for eternity.

The second reading reinforces the truth that people come first. Paul writes to Timothy: "I urge that supplications, prayers, intercessions, and thanksgivings be made for everyone, for kings and all who are in high positions, so that we may lead a quiet and peaceable life in all godliness and dignity. This is right and is acceptable in the sight of God our Saviour, who desires everyone to be saved and to come to the knowledge of the truth."

All that glitters isn't gain. True gain consists in putting people first, ahead of all the goods of this world, and in recognizing that the ultimate value of people is their destiny to an eternal life with God, where they will "come to the knowledge of the truth."

1. Share an experience of money or material things being put ahead of people.
2. What struck you in the gospel reading? What action could you take as a result?
3. In the second reading, Paul says that God "desires everyone to be saved and to come to the knowledge of the truth." How do you feel when you hear these words?
4. What word or phrase from the readings will you carry with you this week?

Twenty-sixth Sunday in Ordinary Time

Amos 6:1a, 4-7
1 Timothy 6:11-16
Luke 16:19-31

From Rags to Riches

If exposed to excessively loud noise over time, our sense of hearing may be impaired or even lost. If we are wise we take steps to protect our hearing in order to avoid this danger.

But are we equally aware of the danger to our "inner hearing," which is regularly bombarded with materialistic messages? The most important things, the media implies, are seeking earthly pleasures and possessing earthly goods. To escape such false persuasion we need a prophetic shot in the arm. We get one in the readings for this Sunday.

In the first reading, the reluctant farmer-turned-prophet, Amos, speaks to the comfortable rich: "Alas for those who lie on beds of ivory...and eat lambs from the flock, and calves from the stall; who sing idle songs to the sound of the harp...who drink wine from bowls, and anoint themselves with the finest oils, but are not grieved over the ruin of Joseph [Israel]! Therefore they shall now be the first to go into exile."

Harsh words! Riches and comfort can lull the inner hearing so we do not hear the cries of the poor.

In the gospel, Jesus, even more insightfully than Amos, warns us about the dulling danger of wealth. He does this through the parable of the rich man and Lazarus, a poor man.

The rich man had everything; Lazarus had nothing. That is bad enough. But what was worse, the rich man had lost all concern for others. He didn't care a fig about the poverty-stricken Lazarus.

But time caught up, as it always does, with the rich man and with Lazarus. Both died. Lazarus was taken up into the bosom of Abraham (heaven), whereas the rich man entered the torment of Hades (hell). Their conditions were eternally reversed. The rich man, still overbearing, wanted Lazarus to wait upon him, to slake his thirst. No go, said Abraham. Well, then, the rich man said, warn my brothers on earth lest they follow me here. "They have Moses and the prophets," Abraham replied. This isn't enough, the rich man said, "but if someone goes to them from the dead, they will repent." Abraham put him straight. "If they do not listen to Moses and the prophets, neither will they be convinced even if someone rises from the dead."

A telling parable indeed! We all need to ponder it.

The second reading points out clearly where our true riches are. Paul says to Timothy, "But as for you, [Timothy], man of God, shun all this; pursue righteousness, godliness, faith, love, endurance, gentleness. Fight the good fight of the faith; take hold of the eternal life, to which you were called and for which you made the good confession."

These words, addressed to each one of us, point out the only true way to go from rags to riches.

⌐⊛⌐

1. What do you think Amos would say about our lifestyle today?
2. The gospel makes it crystal clear that we are to help "the poor." Who are the poor? How can you help them?
3. How can you follow the advice Paul gives to Timothy (quoted above)?
4. What word or phrase from the readings will you carry with you this week?

Twenty-seventh Sunday
in Ordinary Time

Habakkuk 1:2-3; 2:2-4
2 Timothy 1:6-8, 13-14
Luke 17:5-10

When Things Go Wrong, Hold On!

When things go wrong and there is no clear way to set them right, we are liable to become extremely uptight. For example, the world today is filled with acts of terrorism, thefts, weak economies and unresolved problems. Even our own personal lives sometimes get out of whack. As a result we often end up in a stew of frustration.

But take heart. Even the prophets experienced these kinds of ups and downs, as we see in the first reading for this Sunday. Habakkuk lived at the beginning of the sixth century BC. The times then were not just bad, they were terrible. So Habakkuk complains, "O Lord, how long shall I cry for help, and you will not listen? Or cry to you 'Violence!' and you will not save? Why do you make me see wrongdoing and look at trouble? Destruction and violence are before me; strife and contention arise." Habakkuk speaks very plainly!

And what answer does God give? "There is still a vision for the appointed time…. If it seems to tarry, wait for it; it will surely come, it will not delay." In other words, God tells Habakkuk to hold on. God knows the world's messes better than we do. Human free will is to have its way. But, as Paul says, "We know that all things work together for good for those who love God." (Romans 8:28)

Both the second reading and the gospel reinforce and refine God's answer to the frustrated Habakkuk.

Paul writes to Timothy, "Hold to the standard of sound teaching that you have heard from me, in the faith and love that are in Christ Jesus. Guard the good treasure entrusted to you, with the help of the Holy Spirit living in us."

In the gospel, the apostles ask Jesus to "increase our faith!" Jesus replies, "If you had faith the size of a mustard seed, you could say to this mulberry tree, 'Be uprooted and planted in the sea,' and it would obey you."

Now a mulberry tree is known for its deep roots. It is very difficult to uproot it. Besides, how can you plant a tree in the sea? Evidently Jesus was telling the apostles, and us, that what is impossible for us is not impossible for God. The message again is "hold on."

The gospel concludes with a gentle dig at our human pretensions before God. Jesus says, "Do you thank the slave for doing what was commanded? So you also, when you have done all that you were ordered to do, say, 'We are worthless slaves; we have done only what we ought to have done!'"

The point Jesus makes is that when all is said and done, the day is won not by our works but by God's power. So when we are frustrated, we must hold on and hang in! God is at work. No matter how sorry the picture, God's power can, and will, make it right.

❦

1. Share an experience of frustration and how it worked out.
2. God has a vision for us and for our universe. How would you put this vision into words?
3. Paul tells us in the second reading to hold on to sound teaching and to do so in the faith and love that are in Christ Jesus. How does Luke, in the gospel, give you the courage to do so, especially in Jesus' words about the mulberry tree?
4. In the gospel, Jesus puts us in our place. How does this make you feel?

Twenty-eighth Sunday in Ordinary Time

2 Kings 5:14-17
2 Timothy 2:8-13
Luke 17:11-19

The Depth of the Gift Is in the Giver

This phrase refers to a very common but meaningful experience in human life. You receive a gift – on your birthday, at Christmas, on an anniversary. How do you feel? Do your eyes see only the gift? Or do you see in the gift the loving thoughtfulness of the giver?

This very human experience forms the heart of this Sunday's readings.

A Syrian, Naaman, came to Israel in search of the prophet Elisha, whom he hoped would cure him of leprosy. Elisha received him and told him to immerse himself in the River Jordan seven times. At first Naaman was reluctant. The River Jordan was just a muddy stream. It didn't seem a likely place to be cured of leprosy. Nevertheless, he finally did as Elisha had commanded and was cured.

Naaman's reaction to this gift was to say, "Now I know that there is no God in all the earth except in Israel."

Naaman saw through the gift to the giver, the Lord of Israel. Indeed, he asked Elisha if he might take two muleloads of Israelite soil back to Syria. He planned to build an altar for sacrifice on this soil because, as he said, "your servant will no longer offer burnt offering or sacrifice to any god except the Lord."

The gospel is also about leprosy. Ten lepers came to Jesus and cried out, "Jesus, Master, have mercy on us!" Jesus did. He told them to go and show themselves to the priest (who alone could pronounce someone cured of leprosy). On the way to the priest the ten found themselves healed. Only one, however – a Samaritan – returned to thank Jesus.

Only the heretical and despised Samaritan found the depth of the gift. Only he found Jesus. The other nine saw Jesus only as a wonder worker who healed them. But the Samaritan realized who Jesus was: the Messiah and Saviour. To him only did Jesus say, "Get up and go on your way; your faith has made you well." Ten lepers were outwardly healed but only one was healed inwardly.

The second reading concentrates on Jesus, the giver and the gift. "Remember Jesus Christ," Paul writes to Timothy, "raised from the dead." Further on Paul says, "If we have died with him, we will also live with him; if we endure, we will also reign with him."

The depth of all the gifts we receive is the risen Jesus. To stop short at the gifts we receive and revel only in them is to miss out on the real gift, who is Jesus. He gave himself for us and to us. He continues to offer himself to us at every moment of every day. He alone is the gift who leads us to the fullness of life.

⌒❀⌒

1. Share an example from your own life of seeing the giver in the gift.
2. Recall a time when you reacted like Naaman before and after his cure.
3. We would all like to identify with the one leper who returned to give thanks to Jesus. But in all honesty can we do so? How can we become more like this thankful person?
4. Share some of your own experiences of growing into a deeper relationship with Jesus.

Twenty-ninth Sunday in Ordinary Time

Exodus 17:8-13
2 Timothy 3:14–4:2
Luke 18:1-8

Promises, Promises and "the" Promise

Promises in the business world are not always what they are cracked up to be. We have all been disappointed at times with a product or service that didn't live up to a company's promises. Even our personal promises may fall short in the wear and tear of daily life. "Until death do us part," so sincerely meant, sometimes ends in the divorce court.

In the first reading, from the book of Exodus, Israel enters into battle for the first time in its young history. Its way to the Promised Land is thwarted by the Amalekite raiders. Moses orders his general, Joshua, to oppose them. Joshua does. Meanwhile, as the battle rages, Moses looks down on the battle from a hilltop. "Whenever Moses held up his hand, Israel prevailed; and whenever he lowered his hand, Amalek prevailed." So Moses' companions seat him on a rock and support his arms themselves, thus assuring victory.

God was faithful to his promise. The Amalekites could not stop Israel's progress to their destiny.

In the gospel, Jesus tells the parable of the unjust judge and his persistent client, a widow. She was seeking judgment against her enemy, but the judge wasn't about to give in to her. Because she kept after him until he finally helped her, Jesus says, "Will not God grant justice to his chosen ones who cry to him day and night? Will he delay long in helping them? I tell you, God will quickly grant justice to them."

God is always faithful in answering our prayers, although the answers may not be quite what we expect. What delays there may be form part of our training.

The second reading points to one of the great sources of strength for our prayer life. Paul tells Timothy, "Continue in what you have learned and firmly believed." Then he adds these profound words: "All scripture is inspired by God and is useful for teaching, for reproof, for correction, and for training in righteousness, so that everyone who belongs to God may be proficient, equipped for every good work."

God's word is indispensable to us. Without it, our prayer life would wither and die.

At the very end of the gospel, Jesus says, "And yet, when the Son of Man comes, will he find faith on earth?" He will, provided you and I continue to be nourished by God's word. For that word helps sustain us in a loving relationship with God and our neighbour. Moreover, it continually reminds us of *the* promise: that God will lead us to eternal life.

1. Share an experience of receiving an answer to your prayers.
2. Describe an experience of asking God for a favour but receiving an altogether different favour that turns out to be more precious than the one you asked for.
3. What can you do when God seems to turn a deaf ear to your requests?
4. How can reflecting on God's word in the sacred Scriptures offer you consolation?

Thirtieth Sunday in Ordinary Time

Sirach 35:15-17, 20-22
2 Timothy 4:6-8, 16-18
Luke 18:9-14

False-Fronting Doesn't Pay Off

All of us must admit, if we are honest, that we do a good deal of false-fronting. We are inclined to put our best foot forward while concealing the other foot's limp as best we can. Put another way, we hide our weaknesses, our shortcomings, our failings. We seldom allow "the real me" to appear.

Trying to fool others is bad enough. It's even worse to try to fool ourselves. Worst of all, however, is trying to fool God. We seldom fool others with our false fronts. Even less do we fool ourselves. But never, ever, do we fool God. This is abundantly clear in this Sunday's readings.

As the first reading puts it, "The Lord is the judge, and with him there is no partiality." He sees into the depths of the human heart. Only the sincere are acceptable to him. "The one whose service is pleasing to the Lord will be accepted," Sirach says, and "the prayer of such a person will reach to the clouds."

Paul, in the second reading, begins with what seems to be a boast. "I have fought the good fight, I have finished the race, I have kept the faith." This wasn't boasting. Paul was simply stating the direction his life took after meeting the risen Jesus on the road to Damascus. As his life drew to a close he looked ahead, putting his trust in God and expressing the hope that God would give him "a crown of righteousness." Paul knew that a crown would also be given "to all who have longed for his appearing."

Paul also knew that it wasn't his own strength that enabled him to follow Christ and put his hope in a crown of righteousness. Rather, as he acknowledges at the end of the second reading, "The Lord will rescue me from every evil attack and save me for his heavenly kingdom. To him be the glory forever and ever. Amen."

The gospel tells the story of "two men [who] went up to the temple to pray, one a Pharisee and the other a tax collector." We know the story well. The Pharisee, standing by himself, thanked God he wasn't like some other people and then proceeded to list his many virtues. The tax collector, standing at the back, didn't even feel worthy enough to raise his eyes to God but kept "beating his breast and saying, 'God, be merciful to me, a sinner!'" Jesus says, "I tell you, this man went back home justified rather than the other."

False-fronting doesn't pay off. Honesty to others, with ourselves and before God does pay off – and handsomely.

1. Give a few examples of "false-fronting" from your own life.
2. What makes a truly humble person? How can you recognize this quality in others and in yourself?
3. In light of the gospel, share further thoughts on false-fronting and on humility.
4. What word or phrase from the readings will you carry with you this week?

Thirty-first Sunday in Ordinary Time

Wisdom 11:22–12:2
2 Thessalonians 1:11–2:2
Luke 19:1-10

You Are a Walking Miracle

Have you seen the Emmy-award winning film *The Woman Who Willed a Miracle*? In it May Lemka, an English nurse, came to the United States, where she worked in a hospital for people with serious health problems. One of the patients was a little boy, Leslie. He was so severely afflicted that eventually all the staff gave up on him. All, that is, except May. She took him into her own home and eventually adopted him.

For years, despite all the help May gave him, Leslie was unable to feed himself, stand alone or speak. Then one night May and her husband heard classical music coming from the parlour. Thinking they had left the radio on, they went into the parlour. To their utter astonishment, they saw that it was Leslie playing the piano. That was the big breakthrough. From then on, his rehabilitation occurred rapidly. Eventually he became a renowned concert pianist. A true miracle!

In the first reading, the author of the book of Wisdom praises God for showing such awesome power: "The whole world before you, O Lord, is like a speck that tips the scales." Yet this awesome God is "merciful to all" and loves "all things that exist." This God also is one who overlooks people's sins.

In the second reading, Paul prays that God will make his Thessalonian converts "worthy of his call and will fulfill by his power every good resolve."

In the gospel, Jesus, on entering Jericho, looks up and sees Zacchaeus, the tax collector of the district, up in a tree. Immediately he calls out, "Zacchaeus, hurry and come down; for I must stay at your house today." As a result of their encounter, Zacchaeus underwent a complete conversion.

The main point of the three readings is that despite our unworthiness God calls us, forgives us and nurtures us to spiritual well-being. God never has, and never will, give up on anyone. Such is God's creative love. Thus each of us is indeed a walking miracle.

1. How do you see God's tender but awesome power in creation?
2. Share experiences of God's love in your life.
3. We are yet in God's womb, and so is our universe. How do you understand God's call for further growth?
4. Share your own way of expressing that we are all "walking miracles."

Thirty-second Sunday in Ordinary Time

2 Maccabees 7:1-2, 9-14
2 Thessalonians 2:16–3:5
Luke 20:27-38

"Ours Is the Better Choice"

In the film *Romero,* which tells the story of Archbishop Oscar Romero of El Salvador, a supporting character named Lucia foresees that her continuing struggle for freedom may end up in personal tragedy. She asks a priest who is also involved in the struggle whether it is all worthwhile. She wonders if there really is an afterlife. If not, why keep up the fight for freedom? Yet she chooses to continue the fight, knowing what that choice means. Eventually her fears are realized, and she is murdered for her beliefs.

In our own country, we do not face the choice Lucia faced. But we do have to choose whether to follow Christ or simply to eat, drink and be merry. This Sunday's readings can help us as we face this choice.

The first reading tells of seven brothers who, with their mother, were arrested for resisting the Syrians. Unfortunately for the Syrians, they picked the wrong people to hold up as examples. The entire family chose to die rather than disobey the laws of their ancestors.

When the second brother came to die, he said to those who were about to kill him, "You dismiss us from this present life, but the King of the universe will raise us up to an everlasting renewal of life."

In the second reading, Paul urges his Thessalonian converts to pray "that we may be rescued from wicked and evil people…. But the Lord is faithful; he will strengthen you and guard you from the evil one."

In the gospel we meet the Sadducees, a sect of Jewish people who did not believe in angels or in the resurrection of the dead. To trap Jesus, they put to him the case of the seven brothers who, following the leviratic law, each in turn married the same woman on the death of their brother. The Sadducees asked, "In the resurrection, therefore, whose wife will the woman be? — for the seven had married her."

Jesus replied that marriage is for this life, not the next. Then he went on to make the point that in one of the books that the Sadducees accepted as inspired, Moses calls the Lord "the God of Abraham, the God of Isaac, and the God of Jacob." Jesus then drew this conclusion: "Now he is God not of the dead, but of the living; for to him all of them are alive." Therefore, Jesus implies, Abraham, Isaac and Jacob must be alive.

There is, then, a resurrection to new life.

Since there is resurrection to new life, ours is the better choice when we opt to follow Christ and not the world.

1. Describe a time when you were put on the spot because of your faith.
2. Have you ever been strengthened by the truth of the resurrection? What happened?
3. Paul once wrote that as in Adam we all die, so in Christ we all come to life. Reflect on this profound truth.
4. What word or phrase from the readings will you carry with you this week?

Thirty-third Sunday in Ordinary Time

Malachi 4:1-2
2 Thessalonians 3:7-12
Luke 21:5-19

An Agenda for End-Time, but No Timetable

Twiddling our thumbs will not solve a problem. Nor will being overwhelmed by the immensity of the problem. Rather, we need to face it openly and think it through clearly.

Thinking about the end of the world – with all its scary ramifications and its fiery imagery – is disturbing! We may feel paralyzed by the whole concept. Fortunately, the writers of Scripture can bring clarity to the matter, as we see in this Sunday's readings.

In the first reading, the prophet Malachi meets some Israelites, still not settled in their return from exile, who insist that evildoers are winning the day. They wonder, what's the use of continuing in the way of faith? Malachi meets their objection head on: "See, the day is coming, burning like an oven, when all the arrogant and all evildoers will be stubble…. But for you who revere my name the sun of righteousness shall rise, with healing in its wings."

In other words, Malachi was saying, go about doing good work and don't be overawed by the success of evildoers. In the long run you'll succeed and they won't. Your work will pay off eternally; theirs will go up in smoke.

In the second reading, Paul addresses those Thessalonian converts who think that since end-time is just around the corner, it's useless to keep working. Paul doesn't know when end-time will come but he is sure that until it comes, the followers of Christ must earn their daily bread. Paul himself did. He advises the Thessalonians to do the same and not use end-time as an excuse for laziness.

While Mark and Matthew combine their accounts on the end of the temple and the end of Jerusalem and the end of the world, Luke separates the three. In this Sunday's gospel, Luke speaks of the destruction of the temple. Reacting to his followers' comment on the beauty of the temple, Jesus says, "As for these things that you see, the days will come when not one stone will be left upon another; all will be thrown down."

When the disciples ask when this destruction will take place, Jesus answers that first there will be many catastrophes and persecutions. Luke wants us to realize that just as there is to be distress before the destruction of the temple, and of Jerusalem, so there will be distress before the end of the world. Jesus tries to lessen the disciples' fears, saying, "You will be hated by all because of my name. But not a hair of your head will perish. By your endurance you will gain your souls."

There is then no timetable for end-time, but there is a clear agenda: we are to go about our daily task of loving God and our neighbour and all that such love entails, and leave the rest to God. The end may be tomorrow or it may be a million years away. No matter. It will come. Today remains a time of preparation. That is the task at hand.

~❀~

1. How does the prophet Malachi help us face up to end-time?
2. St. Gerard, when asked what he would do were end-time to occur that very day, replied, "I would keep on with the work I am doing." What do you think of this answer?
3. Recall Paul's words in the second reading. How do you deal with people who predict the exact time of Jesus' final coming?
4. In Jesus' day, Jewish people connected end-time with the destruction of the temple. What is your understanding of the advice Jesus gives to his followers?

Christk the King

2 Samuel 5:1-3
Colossians 1:12-20
Luke 23:35-43

Serving with Authority

"Power corrupts," the saying goes. Time has proven this to be true. There is simply too much selfishness at the core of our human nature for us to withstand the lure of power. Those in authority often end up abusing their power. They use it for their own gain and for the gain of those close to them.

This stands as a warning to us all. For we all wield some authority, if not through the office we hold, then at least through the gifts we possess. (Gifts are a form of power.) How are we to overcome this corrupting power of authority? The readings for this Sunday, the Feast of Christ the King, point the way.

The first reading explains that "all the tribes of Israel came to David at Hebron.... King David made a covenant with them at Hebron before the Lord, and they anointed David king over Israel."

By and large, David proved to be a good king. Yet he abused his authority in causing the death of Uriah, a soldier, so he could have Uriah's wife.

The kings who succeeded David, with few exceptions, were not good kings. They brashly abused their authority. But one king of David's line, Jesus of Nazareth, did not abuse his authority. Rather, he became the servant of all.

In the second reading, Paul reminds the Colossians of what God has done for them (and for all of us) through Christ Jesus. The Father "has rescued us from the power of darkness and transferred us into the kingdom of his beloved Son, in whom we have redemption, the forgiveness of sins." Jesus was jeered on the cross, as Luke tells us; the soldiers mocked him; and over his head a sign read "This is the King of the Jews." One of the thieves crucified beside him rebuked Jesus for not saving them. The other thief, however, said to him, "'Do you not fear God, since you are under the same sentence of condemnation? And we indeed have been condemned justly...but this man has done nothing wrong.' Then he said, 'Jesus, remember me when you come into your kingdom.' Jesus replied, 'Truly I tell you, today you will be with me in Paradise.'"

Jesus, a king, was a servant to the very end. Like him, we must use our authority humbly and for the good of those who come under our influence.

1. Share your experience of serving with power (e.g., as a parent, in your job, through a talent you possess).
2. In the second reading, Paul describes the power of Jesus and then says that the Church is the body of Jesus. What conclusions can you draw from this great truth?
3. Luke's words in the gospel are very heartening. What strikes you most about them? In particular, share your reactions to Jesus' promise to the good thief.
4. What word or phrase from the readings will you carry with you this week?

Also Available from Novalis

Preparing for Sunday
Exploring the Readings for Year A
(Available in Fall 2004)

Preparing for Sunday
Exploring the Readings for Year B

Fr. John Spicer CSsR offers faith-filled reflections on the readings for individuals and groups.

The Living with Christ Sunday Missal

The *Living with Christ Sunday Missal* helps Catholics prepare for and participate more fully in the Sunday liturgy. Contains complete readings and mass texts, as well as selected hymns, for all Sundays and feast days. The perfect companion to *Preparing for Sunday*!

To order, call 1-877-702-7773
or visit our Web site:
www.novalis.ca

Fr. John Spicer CSsR is director emeritus of the Adult Learning Commission of the Archdiocese of Edmonton, Alberta. He is a well-known and frequent contributor to the Catholic press, especially in western Canada. His *Preparing for Sunday* series continues with separate volumes for Years A and B.

CARNAL KNOWLEDGE

essential SEX trivia

CARNAL KNOWLEDGE

THE EROTIC PRINT SOCIETY/MOONDANCE MEDIA
LONDON 2005

The Erotic Print Society
17 Harwood Road
London SW6 4QP
Orderline (UK only): 0800 026 25 24
Fax: +44 (0)20 7736 6330
Email: eros@eroticprints.org
Web: www.eroticprints.org

Moondance Media Ltd
9 Harmsworth Street, Kennington
London SE17 3TJ
Tel: +44 (0)20 7820 8844
Fax: +44 (0)20 7820 9944
Email: desire@moondancemedia.co.uk
Web: www.desire.co.uk

Printed and bound in Spain by IGOL, Barcelona

ISBN: 1-904989-12-8

MOONDANCE MEDIA

EPS

contributors
Ian Jackson
Ian Lowey
Jamie Maclean
Jo Perryman
Suzy Prince
Lesley Ann Sharrock
Charlie Webb
Saskia Vogel

edited by
Ian Jackson

many thanks to
Sara Backhouse, John Forsyth, Joe Harrison,
Sylvie Jones, Tim Major, Robert McGinley,
Gloria Perryman, Ronald Putzker, Paul
Rivers, Gordon Rondelle, Charles
Simmonds and the Rare crew.

We cannot guarantee the accuracy
of the information contained
within. Please send any
corrections that are needed,
as well as the source
where we can verify
the corrections.

CONTENTS

INTRODUCTION

It's said that we think about sex every 7 minutes – or was it 4 minutes, or 11 minutes, or 23 minutes... It's no surprise, then, that sex is the world's favourite subject and manages to make its way into most facets of our lives. And if, like most people, you enjoy sex, you'll probably also be intrigued by it all.

Carnal Knowledge has been put together by a group of people who have laboured long and hard in the adult industry for their sins. In that time, they've accumulated a wealth of information about every imaginable aspect of sex.

Packed with entertaining and genuinely useful stuff, this compact book should provide hours of diverting browsing. And the info within will always come in handy during lulls in the chat on those Friday nights in the pub, or when the dinner-party conversation turns to mortgages and pensions.

Of course, *Carnal Knowledge* doesn't promise you a great sex life or to make you a better person, but you'll almost certainly be the richer for knowing that little bit more about the wonderful and often bizarre world of sex, its quirks, its history and its outrageous myths and truths.

And if you originally considered this volume as a gift for someone else, once you've started reading, you just might want to keep it for yourself.

THE ULTIMATE
SWINGERS' LOVE-IN

In July 2006, the Stardust Resort & Casino in Las Vegas will host the 33rd annual swingers convention, organised by the Lifestyles Organisation. If you think that the swinging scene peaked in the Seventies, think again. In 2005, over five days, around 3,000 couples from across the USA and the rest of the world gathered for the planet's biggest swingers' shindig.

This hedonistic celebration of sexual freedom included moonlight pool parties; a Ms Lifestyles and a Mr Buns competition; a 100-booth Adult Fantasy Market Place and a massage workshop.

The seminar programme featured 'The Elusive G-Spot', 'Ancient Lovemaking Secrets', 'Erotic Art Survey', 'Sensual Rope Bondage', 'Corseting in the New Millennium', and 'A Couple's Guide to XXX Videos'.

In addition, there were four gala dances, each with a different theme: Naughty Girls Nite, Taboo Tiki Beach Party, Bikers & Babes, and Feather Fantasies Masquerade Ball.

And if that wasn't enough, swing clubs from around the country also hosted parties in various suites. But what would a swingers' jamboree be without an orgy? Well, they managed to fit in a couple of those, too – held in the Vegas resort's Presidential Suite with half a dozen rooms on two levels, complete with a bar. You can almost hear the ghost of Ol' Blue Eyes crooning 'Strangers in the Night'...
www.Lifestyles-Convention.com

PORNO SUPERSTAR

Jenna Jameson has achieved true porno superstar status and has been honoured with more awards than any other performer in the history of adult entertainment. And not only has Jenna successfully maintained a twelve-year career at the top in a business notorious for its high turnover of talent, but she's also one of the few hardcore actresses to have crossed over into the mainstream. And her recent autobiography, *How to Make Love Like a Porn Star* even made the *New York Times*' best sellers list.

Born in Las Vegas in 1974, Jenna began her career as a dancer at a strip club in her home city. By the age of twenty, she was baring all in magazines such as *Hustler* and *Penthouse*, and she made her adult movie debut in 1993. Two

years later, she signed a lucrative contract with Wicked Pictures which allowed her unprecedented control over the number of movies she made, who she appeared with, and which sex acts she performed. She has appeared in over 200 porn movies to date and, though Jenna has worked with men, she seemingly prefers girl-on-girl scenes and still resolutely refuses to do anal.

Today Jenna is the head of ClubJenna Inc, through which she now produces her own movies, licensed and distributed via American market leaders Vivid Entertainment. ClubJenna also oversees Jameson-related merchandise such as pube-trimmers and life-size Jenna love dolls. Now, who was it that said women in pornography are exploited?

Minks have intercourse that lasts an average of eight hours.

Averaging three seconds, the chimpanzee holds the record for the quickest mammal sexual intercourse.

A pig's penis is shaped like a corkscrew.

Most turkeys and giraffes are bisexual.

An adult gorilla's penis is a mere two inches long.

Wild animals, as a rule, don't get sexually transmitted diseases, but otters can get herpes.

Humans and porpoises both practise group sex – but not together!

Humans, fish and porpoises all practise fellatio.

A rhinoceros's penis is two feet long on average.

After or even during sex, the Black Widow spider eats her mate.

A single ejaculation from a bull can inseminate 300 cows.

Mouse sperm is longer than elephant sperm.

The female bedbug has no sexual opening; thus, the male drills a vagina into the female with his curved penis.

The blue whale has the world's largest penis, at three metres long.

Some lions mate over 50 times daily.

Male bats have the highest rate of homosexuality of any mammal.

The raccoon penis has a little bone in it that has been used as a toothpick by some.

Most male birds don't have a penis, but rather holes that pass the sperm to the females.

When a male deer rubs his antlers on a tree, it is a form of masturbation.

A pig's orgasm lasts for 30 minutes.

The penguin has only one single, solitary orgasm in a whole year. Aah...

IT'S SEX, JIM, BUT NOT AS WE KNOW IT...

FOOT NOTES

While the TV series, *Sex & the City*, may have made Manolo Blahnik a byword for sassy women's shoes, many hotly argue that the ultimate in 'fuck-me' shoes are made by Gina, Jimmy Choo or Christian Louboutin (with their trademark scarlet soles).

When porno superstar Jenna Jameson was recently asked what she felt was her most attractive feature, she simply removed her shoes to reveal her pretty and very petite tootsies. Back in the 1930s, film director DW Griffiths *(Birth of a Nation)* organised a competition to find women with the most beautiful feet. The winner's name is lost and forgotten, but the runner-up was Hollywood star, Joan Crawford.

In the 1980s, when Ferdinand Marcos, then president of the Philippines, was deposed, he and his wife Imelda fled the country, leaving behind her cherished collection of designer shoes, only later discovered in the royal palace. She had accumulated over 3,000 pairs: that makes for noo shooz every single day for more than eight years.

The shoes pictured here, designed by Stuart Weitzman, were modelled on Dorothy's red slippers from *The Wizard of Oz*. They're woven from platinum thread and set with 642 rubies, and went on sale in Harrods in 2002 for the fairy-tale price of £1,000,000.

> I don't know who invented the high heel, but all women owe him a lot
>
> Marilyn Monroe

Fashion writer, Valerie Steele, once described sandals as 'the sexiest of shoe styles, because they leave the foot nearly naked', and the straps, which suggest bondage, 'present the foot as a beautiful slave'.

Perhaps this goes some way to explain why Western society – from the ancient Romans to the Puritans – regarded the naked foot as impure and shameful, and decreed that respectable women should cover their feet. Saint Jerome advised women to wear shoes that would conceal the entire foot, to 'subdue the carnal inclinations lurking in men's eyes'.

And Saint Clement urged that women should not bare their toes in public, and strongly disapproved of 'the mischievous device of sandals that evokes temptations'.

Even in 1939, *Vogue* magazine declared that sandals were just too revealing to be worn on the street, as they had 'neither toes nor backs, just heels and straps'.

ROOM SERVICE
EXTREME MAKE-OVER

Move over 'Changing Rooms'. Here are some tips for transforming your bedroom into a temple of lust:

■ Raunchy music will always help to get you in the mood for lurve.

■ Buy in some candles (preferably scented) for a really seductive atmosphere. Take care, though: you might want to set the bed on fire, but... (Candles can also be put to good use by dripping hot wax on each other. This is one of those things – you'll either love it or hate it, so go easy at first.)

■ Keep your bedside cabinet well stocked with goodies close to hand: sex toys and accoutrements, plus lubes and condoms.

■ Cushions are essential for avoiding carpet burns on knees or bums, when the action is not confined to the bed.

■ A large mirror adds a voyeuristic dimension to your sex antics. Those full-length free-standing ones that tilt are just the ticket. Mirrors on the ceiling can be a bit OTT, and you can't turn them away when you feel like it.

■ An ice bucket comes in handy for keeping your champagne chilled, certainly. But the ice cubes can also be used in a fair number of cool and sexy ways...

■ And a selection of adult DVDs on the TV to spur you on to emulate the full-on sexual gymnastics on screen.

MEET THE **REAL** McCOY

On regular business trips to Germany, **George McCoy** was impressed by the wide variety of adult entertainment and services on offer in cities such as Frankfurt and Hamburg, and the number of detailed guidebooks providing copious info about the adult scene for visitors.

And so *McCoy's British Massage Parlour Guide*, with star ratings for each establishment, was launched in 1996. The guide immediately generated media coverage, which led to after-dinner speaking engagements, magazine articles and a number of TV appearances.

His range of guides now include *McCoy's Street Plans for Men*, highlighting locations of parlours, escorts, sex shops, adult parties and strip clubs in Manchester, Birmingham and London.

On his endless odyssey checking out premises for each updated edition, he has befriended some memorable characters along the way: Tina the Russian Dynamo, Tammy the Tiger, Jessica the Pencil-thin Redhead Superstar, Athletic Andrea, Lady Penelope, Legs Lauren and Lips Lauren.

And nowadays, McCoy's guides are referred to by working girls themselves, to determine which establishments provide the best working conditions and facilities!

He always ventures out in his distinctive flat cap, yet over the years, it seems many blokes have tried to pass themselves off as McCoy, and to his chagrin, he has become an iconic figure to scores of chavs who greet him enthusiastically, 'Let me shake you by the hand, George. You're my hero!'

Yes, it's a tough job providing the unvarnished low-down on Britain's sex establishments, and thankfully McCoy is there to do it...
www.mccoysguide.com

SEX MYTHS EXPLODED

OK, so we know masturbation doesn't make you go blind, but it seems some sex myths and urban legends continue to live on in the popular imagination. So we though we'd debunk a few, once and for all.

Feminists burned their bras.
This story originated from the 1968 Miss America beauty pageant in Atlantic City, USA. It was reported that a group of feminists, protesting against the event, had burned their bras. Only they weren't actually burned, but rather binned. Amazing how a whole myth can be sparked by a simple typographical error.

Swingers select their partners for the night by having the ladies pluck car keys, lucky-dip style, from a bowl. The man whose keys are chosen duly pairs off with the lady who picked them.
This exact scenario was played out recently in a rather smug car advert for Toyota. A similar 'key party' scene was used in the 1997 movie, *The Ice Storm*, and the notion of swingers choosing their partners this way seems to have been a staple of sensationalised Sunday tabloid 'wife swapping' exposes. But despite all of this, Bob McGinley of NASCA (North American Swing Clubs Association) states categorically that swingers have never selected partners that way, and many veteran British swingers say they've never encountered the method either.

Prince Albert had the erotic piercing to which he gave his name.
It's commonly held that Queen Victoria's beloved husband Prince Albert had a ring pierced through the end of his penis, in order to secure it to a hook on the inside of his trousers, so as not to spoil their line. Though it's difficult to prove one way or the other, there are no valid historical accounts to support the story, which is said by many to have been made up in the 1970s by the Californian piercing pioneer, Doug Malloy.

Pornography generates more revenue than the entire entertainment industry (including film, music and sport).

It seems to us that, when reporting on pornography, journalists are suddenly struck with an inexplicable willingness to completely suspend disbelief. Unquestioningly, they are happy to regurgitate the same astounding 'facts' about the gigantic scale of the adult industry. Partly, this is down to the fact that such notions tie in nicely with the anti-porn arguments of most media writers, supporting the idea that society is being swamped by pernicious filth. But the simple truth is that, when an average XXX video might be expected to shift 1,000–5,000 copies in the United States, sales of 20,000 copies make it a runaway best-seller. Compare that with sales of *The Incredibles*: which sold five million DVDs in the USA – in one week!

Catherine the Great was crushed to death having sex with her horse.

Utter piffle. Catherine the Great actually died in bed at the age of 67, after having suffered a stroke (some say whilst she was on the loo). The myth about her having sex with horses was seemingly spread by French revolutionaries, after Catherine had condemned the execution of Marie Antoinette. It was also suggested – again by the French – that Catherine was so randy that even the entire Russian imperial guard couldn't satisfy her. In actual fact, Catherine did enjoy a lusty sex life, but is known to have had just two husbands and eleven lovers in her life, though she is said to have had 'relations' with several guardsmen.

Children's TV series *Captain Pugwash* featured such salty characters as Master Bates, Seaman Staines and Roger the Cabin Boy.

This is perhaps one of the most enduring urban myths of recent times, and even *The Guardian* was forced into issuing an apology after it alleged the BBC had axed the show upon belatedly becoming aware of the innuendo-laden names of the crew. In fact, Pugwash's seafaring cohorts were Master Mate (which admittedly sounds like masturbate), Pirate Barnabas, Pirate Willy, Tom the Cabin Boy and Cut-Throat Jake.

■ When semen was first examined under a microscope in 1677, there was much confusion over the small creatures observed wriggling about in the ejaculate. Some believed they might be parasites. In fact, it would be another 150 years before it was discovered that sperm were part of the fertilisation process.

■ **Semen contains more than thirty elements, including vitamin B12, fructose, citric acid, nitrogen and various salts. And cheaper than health shop supplements.**

■ The average amount of semen per ejaculation is 10cc – from which the British pop band derived its name. If you're counting, there are just five calories in a teaspoon of semen. So no excuses, girls.

■ **Semen can shoot anywhere between 12 to 24 inches and travel at 28 miles per hour. That's faster than Linford Christie.**

■ Men will produce the most sperm between the ages of twenty to thirty. In the course of a lifetime, the average male will ejaculate a total of 20 litres of semen.

■ **You are what you eat. Avoid asparagus, as it causes man juice to smell and taste rank. Better to tuck into watermelon, which perfumes the system, for a sweet scent and taste.**

■ The first sperm banks were established in Japan and the USA in 1964. Sperm banks can store semen indefinitely by maintaining it at a temperature of -300F. A regular American sperm donor can earn up to $5,000 a year.

THE WHITE STUFF

ORGIES

Voltaire, having enjoyed his first orgy, was asked if he wanted to take part in another the next evening. He turned down the invitation, adding in his usual succinct way, 'Once, a philosopher; twice, a pervert!'

Orgies often had a religious significance in the ancient world; indeed the word originates from the Greek meaning 'festival of the night', and frenzied nocturnal drinking, dancing and sex would induce a state of quasi-religious hysteria among participants. Dionysian (later Bacchic) orgies, originally girl-only affairs, became so corrupted, acquiring such an unsavoury reputation that the Roman Senate moved to ban them in 186BC.

By contrast, Renaissance orgies were given an official seal of approval: in 1501, Pope Alexander VI's secretary noted in his diary that His Holiness, as well as Cezare and Lucrezia Borgia, looked on as 50 courtesans stripped off after a feast at the Papal Palace. Lighted candles were set down on the floor and naked women crawled on their hands and knees to pick up chestnuts thrown by spectators. After this early peep show, there were prizes of 'cloaks, hose and brooches' for those who had it off with the most prostitutes on the night.

For any sensitive souls that are not prepared to embrace the new and challenging, orgies might be better kept firmly in the world of fantasy.

But once the would-be orgiast has stepped over the threshold, he or she should be ready to give or receive anything that isn't painful or life threatening. But are the nearest things we have to a fully-fledged Bacchanal or Saturnalia – the *échangiste* clubs of Paris or the swingers parties organised in the Home Counties or California – anything but a faint echo of past glories? That's for you to find out...

HEAVENLY BODIES

How the planets affect your sexual and sensual psyche and shape your desires.

Aries *(22 March–20 April)*

She is drawn to anonymous sexual encounters, just to indulge her passion for stimulation and arousal. Her need to be dominant leads her into fiery relationships born out of frenzied physical desire. She needs sexual freedom and a partner who can accept her forceful Yang, or masculine nature.

He craves excitement. He wants quick responses and he wants them now. For him the fantasy, the image, and sexual build-up is the turn-on. He keeps his pleasure for himself, never allowing his partner access to his imagined world so none can get close to his vulnerability. Lacking sensuality he adores the roughness and heat of the moment and is driven to engage in furious passion.

Taurus *(21 April–21 May)*

This woman possesses a powerful sensuality. For her, touch is pure arousal and long, careful foreplay leads to unbridled passion but her partner has to be in tune with her. She would rather masturbate than have a one-night sexual encounter. With a lover she can trust, she will enjoy playing a submissive role, especially one involving oral sex. Hedonism and the delights of the senses are his mantra. Ravish first, then possess later. He enjoys close contact and heavy foreplay and feels natural naked. Earthy, instinctive and temperamental he gets off on not being in control. He is the serene sensualist who insists on using all five senses.

Gemini *(22 May–22 June)*

Constantly searching for a sexual 'twin', she requires variety but becomes bored with physical contact that does not involve an intellectual element. Dirty talk excites but she avoids too much emotional involvement for fear of getting hurt.

Impulsive and childlike, he will go along with roleplay and kinky sex if asked to but will not initiate. A lover of erotic imagery, he needs a lot of stimulation and communication to keep him interested.

Cancer *(23 June–23 July)*

She projects an aura of total feminine mystique. Her nature is deeply emotional. She is highly sexual and receptive, but masks her powerfully seductive aura with a cloak of controlled worldliness. Yet, beneath this veneer, lies a darkly sensitive and powerfully sensual female; a sexuality that rests mysteriously between pure mental stimulus and complete sensual arousal. He is a sensualist, who indulges in his fantasy world with ease if the ambience is right. It is not excitement, not fiery noisy adventure, that arouses him, but the darkness of his own inner self and the unknown. When turned on enough he will want to dominate and have control over his lover's orgasm.

Leo *(24 July–24 August)*

She is passionate, proud and courageous but self-indulgent and vain. Her lover must view her as the ultimate woman, the sex symbol, the femme fatale, the icon and totem of female sensuality and pleasuring. His loyalty is paramount. She does not require unusual sex aids or role-playing, just glamorous and romantic fantasy.

He is passionate about himself. He enjoys his own control. He needs to be entertained. He fears rejection, criticism or scorn. He lives ▶

HEAVENLY BODIES

though physical reality, rather than the heart and emotions. His lover must boost his ego and sexual esteem regularly or he'll be off. He needs to possess and claim ownership, yet be free to roam.

Virgo *(23 August–23 September)*

Despite her conventional image, she emits an aura and mystique which stems from her sensual soul. She has an insatiable curiosity which can only be satisfied when she acknowledges her earthy inner self. Her self-imposed taboos and defences can be breached by a guilt-free equality of sexual response from a loving partner.

He seeks perfection in others and finds passionate, vocal, dominant women threatening. This man separates emotion from desire, and shuns emotional involvement. He ritualises sexual encounters but becomes more sensual with age, though he expects his partner to devote herself to him in body and in mind.

Libra *(24 September–23 October)*

The ultimate feminine seductress, she seeks out aesthetic pleasure of the mind, not just of the body. She is enchantingly feminine, for illusion and magic are part of her allure as she tempts and teases. Sociable but shy of intimacy, she needs to be chased and captured.

Seeking the ideal sexual fantasy or relationship, he has tenderness, sexual skill and the desire to give but needs intellectual stimulation and erotic conversation first and foremost. He avoids conflict and fears commitment for fear of losing out on a better offer further on up the road.

Scorpio *(24 October–22 November)*

She is mysterious and secretive but very emotional: jealous, passionate and obsessively erotic. She needs to dominate and control,

HEAVENLY BODIES

and can be demanding yet needy. She seeks exotic sexual locations and may be attracted to S&M and bondage.

He has highly potent sexual desires. He wants to possess and ravish and jealousy may be part of arousal for him. Sex for him is symbolic, esoteric and sometimes obsessive. He has a sensual, animal and even sadistic sexual appetite.

Sagittarius *(23 November–22 December)*

She is daring, audacious and liberated and on a quest for spontaneous gratification. She feels sexually comfortable with strangers, acquaintances and the unknown, rather than intimates who might peel away the veneer of independence she so fiercely defends. She is uninhibited and has a demanding sex drive.

Nobody possesses this one. He is hungry for sexual experience. He avoids emotional sex and needs to play games, to amuse himself. His loyalty and honesty is to himself. He has a reputation for promiscuity as his desire is one of adventure and exploration, seeking out new thrills in unusual environments.

Capricorn *(23 December–19 January)*

She is rarely promiscuous and her wisdom and sensuality merge when she is secure with a partner bound to her both physically and emotionally. Then she becomes the wildest of earth women, a being of pure, savage sexuality. Her Yang masculine energy is powerful and she can easily become the aggressor, the dominatrix. Or she may want to be bound to the bedposts while her lover ravishes her.

Though generally sexually dominant, there are two types of Capricorn male; one who is deeply romantic and may have only one partner for life, or the other extreme who may seek out the most dangerous of liaisons. Both types, however need an ambitious and often power-driven woman to match his own thirst for control. ➤

HEAVENLY BODIES

Aquarius *(20 January–19 February)*

Bohemian, cool, glamorous and sophisticated, she is a believer in sexual freedom as an ideology but personally very self-controlled and is more aroused by the idea of sex rather than actual closeness. She is happier in a free-for-all than an intimate relationship where she feels loss of control, and might experiment with group sex and partners of both sexes.

Not one for love or emotional involvement's he fears real sexual intimacy. Flirty, amusing and frivolous, he enjoys detached seduction and playing mind games. He will say what his partners want to hear and he tends to seek out independent women in order to change them.

Pisces *(20 February–21 March)*

This emotional and esoteric yet sensual, elusive and ephemeral woman is driven to attaching herself to both romantic love and sex. She often prefers the company of women to men. Yet she can be drawn to brutish, violent types, She may gather lost and broken souls around her, spending her time in self-denial, so she avoids the pain that she believes is bound with devoted pleasure.

He may drift from pleasure to pleasure, uncertain of what his sexuality is all about. He lives in a fantasy world of romantic eroticism and is drawn to beautiful women. He can become addicted to a partner who treats him with contempt or chooses to dominate him. Yet once involved in a union of love and sex he will be master of erotic excess.

PUSSY POWER

The theatre show, *The Vagina Monologues*, with its changing cast of film stars and celebs has been staged in over 50 countries to date, though it won't be playing in Uganda, where it's been banned.

Sigmund Freud made a big deal about the difference between adolescent clitoral orgasms and the mature woman's vaginal orgasms. Whatever! The clitoris is a woman's only proven orgasmic centre, but plenty of parts of female genitalia stimulate the clit. G-spot, anyone?

The average vagina is 3-6 inches deep and cannot be permanently made looser through penetration. There are no proven cases of vaginal muscles being so strong they can snap a penis or cut off the blood circulation. However, women can train their vaginal muscles to pick up stacks of coins or shoot out ping-pong balls. Kegel exercises train vaginal muscles to contract independently and strengthen the pelvic floor. Squeeze, ladies, squeeze!

Inspired by ancient legends, Freud popularised the myth of the *vagina dentata* (the toothed vagina) linking it to male castration anxiety. Well darlings, the only possibility of an actual fanged pussy is the formation of dermoid cysts, which form only where the skin folds inwards to become another organ and can grow into teeth, bone, or hair.

The vagina, the only self-cleaning organ apart from the eye, has four basic functions: for menstruation; to receive the penis; to hold semen; and as a birth canal.

By the way, the vagina is the internal structure. Including vulva in the definition of vagina is like equating your lips to your throat. The vagina itself is highly insensitive. Makes sense, huh? Especially when women push a watermelon out of a grapefruit-sized opening.

THE BAWDY BARD

Puns, healthily coarse and downright dirty talk are to be found everywhere in William Shakespeare's plays and, of course, there is the open eroticism of the sonnets. His work is extremely sexual, intellectually and physically, and he was never wittier, more given to punning, than when dealing with sex. At every turn you will find explicit Elizabethan sexual slang and innuendo.

So much so that until the late 1960s all editions intended for schools were censored. So there's a fair chance that your set work books were the cleaned-up version.

Glass of virginity, pile for a French velvet, velvet leaves, coun, baldrick, gate, nest of spicery, ring, rose, tail, treasure, Venus glove, dearest bodily part, pillock hill, Netherlands, Spain, constable were all names for female sex organs

Sword, thorn, potato-finger, bauble, dart of love, holy-thistle, pillock, bugle described male sex organs

Bag, purse, damsons were words for testicles

Pick the lock, mount, vault, exchange flesh, fall backwards, plough, thrust to the wall, prick out, tup, make the beast with two backs, kindle, change the cod's head for a salmon's tail, act of shame, act of sport, deed of kindness, yield one's body, pluck a sweet all phrases used to suggest sexual intercourse

Broker, mackerel, pandar were his terms for a pimp

Beagle, Doll Tearsheet, Mistress Kate, hare, guinea-hen, pagan, puzzel, trot, punk, hackney, hobby-horse, bona roba were all descriptions of a prostitute

Resort, leaping house, stew alluded to a brothel

Boggler, play-fellow, paramour, dish, hackney were used for an amorous woman

Bed-presser, juggler, mandrake, mouse-hunt, town-bull, diver, scains-mate referred to a lecher

BIZARRE SEX MACHINES

These are all genuine inventions registered at the US patent office.

Nocturnal Emissions?

Get up before you get off! Fastened around the waist and under the scrotum, this Erection Alarm fits over the flaccid penis. If an erection develops, the lever mechanism sets off an alarm bell.

Pubic Plucker keeps unwanted erections away!

Fasten the clasps to the pubic hair to secure the Plucker over your flaccid penis. If an erection forms, the clasps pull out the pubic hair.

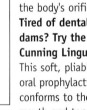

Sex drive driving you crazy?

Deprive yourself of pesky physical contact and easy access to your private bits with Sex Armor!

Sexy satin sheets keeping Johnny up all night?

Get some rest with the Bed Strap. Fit the elastic straps around your neck and knees to keep those naughty bedclothes away from your genitalia.

Nail your attacker with the Tampon of Pain!

This hollow tampon has an internal lacerating spike that will impale the penis upon entry. Reviled by anti-rape campaigners as vengeful and medieval, is this justice or one step too far?

Come already?

The Cock Splint (see pic) keeps you going! Secure underneath the testicles and over the glans. This splint enables a semi-erect or soft penis to penetrate the body's orifices.

Tired of dental dams? Try the Cunning Lingus!

This soft, pliable oral prophylactic conforms to the mouth and tongue to allow for safe oral contact.

Mess-free sex with Menstruator/ Copulator!

The disposable, lubricated vagina-shaped bag adheres to a sanitary pad and lays along the vaginal opening, allowing a man to experience similar sensation to sexual intercourse.

Ride to the valley of delight with the Masterful Mounty!

Pull the elastic harness around your shoulders and mount the base to a fixed object. Hands-free pleasure!

THE **LUST** PICTURE SHOW

■ The first female to appear nude on screen was actress Annette Kellerman, in the 1915 film *Daughter of the Gods*.

■ In 1930, Marlene Dietrich became the first leading lady to kiss another woman on screen in the film *Morocco*.

■ In 1933, *Ecstasy* was the first film to be blocked by US Customs, because of the killer combination of Hedy Lamarr's nude swimming scene, and the close-up of her face during orgasm.

■ Brigitte Bardot introduced the bikini and her pert bottom to the world when she starred in the 1956 film *And God Created Woman*.

■ In 1965, *The Pawnbroker* became the first approved film to reveal a woman's bare breasts: they were deemed an integral part of the story.

■ Bertolucci's 1966 film *Blowup*, is credited as the first mainstream movie in which flashes of pubic hair can be glimpsed.

■ 1967 Swedish film *I am Curious (Yellow)*, contained a nude couple engaged in (simulated) sexual intercourse. The sex-on-screen-starved British public was more than prepared to sit through the arthouse film for a glimpse of flesh on flesh.

■ In 1967 Marianne Faithfull became the first person to say 'fuck' on screen.

■ *Midnight Cowboy* became the only X-rated film ever to win an Oscar for best picture, in 1969.

■ The first sight of an erect penis on British cinema screens came in 1971, courtesy of European arthouse movie *WR: Mysteries of the Organism*. The movie explored the radical theories of the Austrian psychoanalyst Wilhelm Reich, who believed that the release of pent-up aggression through orgasm could free the world of totalitarian oppression!

■ Sharon Stone is perhaps the most high-profile Hollywood actress to have flashed her pussy on screen, as she did in 1992's *Basic Instinct*. Blink and you miss it, though.

■ *The Idiots* contained the first graphic penetration image in a mainstream film, as late as 1998.

■ In 1999, American audiences' view of the orgy scene in *Eyes Wide Shut* was obscured by digitally added figures. European viewers got to see the lot.

■ French film *Baise Moi* provoked a scandal in 2001 when right-wing groups pressurised the French government to reclassify the film as an X, and have it banned from mainstream cinema. It was released uncut in British cinemas but banned in Australia.

■ In 2004, *9 Songs* (above) showed penetration, fellatio, cunnilingus and ejaculation in the most explicit mainstream UK film to date.

DEAD BORING

Necrophilia is defined as the erotic attraction to, or the engagement in sexual activity with, a corpse. Though it's thought to be a rare predisposition, a number of high-profile cases have come to light in recent years, including one which precipitated a change in the law, making sex with corpses illegal in California. Rubber stamped by the Governator, Arnold Schwarzenegger, the bill was thought necessary after an intruder was caught with his pants down in a San Francisco funeral home, having it away with the body of an elderly woman. The man was arrested, but when his case came to court it was discovered that there was nothing in the legislature forbidding sex with a stiff.

Exposed necrophiliacs are almost always males, often working within the funeral industry, which is perhaps why the case of Karen Greenlee caused such a sensation. The infamous American mortician was thought to have have engaged in sexual acts with up to forty newly-deceased males; but her actions had gone unnoticed until she captured the attention of the press and authorities in 1979, after making off in a stolen hearse with the corpse of a young man.

Another notorious, self-confessed female necrophile is Leilah Wendell, who is aroused by sexual encounters with the decayed flesh of buried corpses. Both Wendell – who now runs the American Association of Necrophilic Research and Enlightenment – and Greenlee have to take extraordinary steps to keep their necrophiliac desires under control. Meanwhile, their stories are thought to have been the inspiration behind the Canadian indie movie, *Kissed,* which dealt with the subject of necrophilia quite sensitively, apparently.

NAKED AS NATURE INTENDED

'Adam and Even were naked in the Garden of Eden, and what's good enough for God is good enough for me.' So said the lovely Pamela Green, England's original blonde bombshell. In 1950s Britain, long before the advent of *Penthouse*, there was *Kamera*, a pocket-sized glamour mag created by photographer Harrison Marks and Miss Green.

Brushes with the law, over still pics and 8mm strip flicks that would look playfully wholesome today, made Miss Green Britain's most celebrated (and notorious) nude model. And her alter ego, the exotic redheaded sex siren, Rita Landre, gave her double the modelling work, often in the same magazine, and nobody ever sussed it!

She went on to appear in several nudist B-feature films, gaily throwing beach balls and smiling brightly. But it was perhaps her role in Michael Powell's lurid and controversial 1960 slasher movie, *Peeping Tom*, that secured her a place as a cult icon.

Pamela Green retired from modelling in the late 1970s and today runs a successful website pamela-green.com for her many fans.

A Close Shave
In the 1950s, pubic hair could not be shown in nude glamour photos and so was routinely airbrushed out. Pamela Green got around this by shaving off her pubes, combined with some crafty posing tricks.

BLOWJOBS

As almost anyone can tell you, that greatest misnomer of all time, a blowjob is, in fact, a suck job. So whoever coined this US slang term circa 1940 has a lot to answer for. Generations of enthusiastic oral sex debutantes puffing away and achieving very little, for one…

Even the formal word 'fellatio' comes from the Latin *fellare*, to suck. To give someone a blow-job means to suck and lick his penis and to lick and kiss his balls. Some practitioners are able to 'deep throat', ie control their gagging reflexes and take the entire erect penis deep into their gullet. This requires practice. If the fellatrice causes the man to ejaculate into her mouth she is faced with the real dynamic of the act: swallow or spit.

The 'loving spoonful' is composed of around 2–500 million sperm, making up about 2–5% of the volume of semen. The bulk is composed of seminal plasma, the fluid portion of semen. It appears as a milky-white, viscous fluid, containing water and small amounts of salt, protein, and fructose; the flavour is pretty much indescribable, the texture slightly slimy and cloying, and it has a strong whiff of chlorine. So not everyone wants to swallow. Indeed, as Andy Warhol wrote, 'Everybody I know has a different idea of love. One girl I know said, "I knew he loved me when he didn't come in my mouth"'.

Bad Hair Day
In 1899, French President Faure's mistress, Marguerite Steinheil, was sucking his erect penis when he suddenly had an apoplectic fit and died, his hands apparently grasping her hair in such a tight grip that she had to be cut free. Thereafter she was known as *Pompe Funèbre* (pun of 'funeral industry' and 'deadly sucker').

BLOW**JOBS**

There are plus points to ingesting cum apart from letting your man see you morph from secretary to biker chick in one gulp. Scientists suspect semen can help combat the fellatrice's depression and generally make her feel more chipper as it contains mood-altering hormones. Scottish anatomist John Hunter wrote, 'Semen would appear both by smell and taste to be a mawkish kind of substance; but when held in the mouth it produces a warmth similar to spices.' (Did Mrs Hunter know about this?) And if the taste is too mawkish or the texture too chunky, make your man cut down on unhealthy living.

Pineapple freaks and vegetarians taste great, we are told.
A typical cum-warrior's, er, cocktail might be:
   1 cup pineapple, fresh or tinned
   1 banana
   1 cup apple juice
   2 tsp honey
   1/2 tsp ginger
   1/2 tsp cinnamon
   1/4 tsp nutmeg
   1/2 tsp vanilla extract
Optional ingredients: 1 raw egg white, 2 tps wheat germ.
Combine all ingredients in a blender until smooth. Drink
immediately. Repeat daily for best results.

Believe it or not, until the late 20th century, the clitoris was virtually ignored in medical textbooks. It seems gyneacologists treated it as just a piece of gristle; it was not considered to be involved in reproduction and therefore not pertinent to midwifery! Of course, some might also suggest that men had long sought to downplay the female capacity for sexual pleasure.

The clitoris is the only organ whose sole purpose is to give sexual pleasure. The head of the clitoris contains approximately 8,000 sensory nerve endings, the greatest concentration in the human body.

Just a century ago, Freud still insisted a 'normal' female orgasm should be via the vagina, and not the clitoris!

In the 18th century, a large clitoris was considered abnormal and the possessor suspected of lesbianism and/or instantaneous sex change. In fact, a medical advice book of the time stated: 'If this clytoris chance to grow over-much, it may stand instead of a man's member'.

Back in the 16th century, an Italian doctor, Gabriello Fallopio claimed he had 'identified' the clitoris. And by 1672 a Dutch anatomist, Renier de Graaf, had a very clear understanding of the wishbone structure of the clitoris as his diagrams from the time show. So a fair amount of knowledge was available that long ago.

Today, millions of women across Africa, in predominantly Muslim countries, are denied their right to sexual pleasure. It has been estimated that 100–150 million women have been 'circumcised', a euphemism for the barbaric practice of female genital mutilation, in which the clitoris is removed, often using the most rudimentary equipment (a shard of glass, even) without anaesthetic. In Somalia, for example, 95% of women have had their clitorises removed.

Bud Wiser: Recent studies by Helen O'Connell, a urologist in Melbourne, Australia show that the clitoris is up to nine centimetres long – twice as large as current anatomy books had depicted. And that the little fleshy bud encompasses an upside-down V-shape mass of erectile tissue full of nerves and blood vessels which extends far deeper into the body than anyone suspected. She has noted that medical knowledge of the clitoris was largely based on a few old dissections conducted on older women, where the erectile tissue had shrunk.

CLASSIC CLIT LIT

Women have been responsible for some of the best known classics of erotic literature (or cliterature). There's *Delta of Venus* and *Little Birds*, penned by Anais Nin in the 1930s. Then there's *Emmanuelle*, written by French sexual adventurer, Emmanuelle Arsan. Originally published anonymously, the author of *Story of O* was later revealed to be Pauline Reage. In the early 70s, Erica Jong's *Fear of Flying* introduced us to the 'zipless fuck'. Around the same time a collection of women's sexual fantasies were published as *My Secret Garden* by Nancy Friday. More recent successes have included French bluestocking Catherine Millet's catalogue of sexual encounters, *The Sexual Life of Catherine M*, and the wispy musings of Italian teenager Melissa P, in *One Hundred Stokes of the Brush Before Bed*. And following on in the recent trend for true carnal confessionals, *Belle De Jour* is the anonymously-written diary of a high-class London hooker and *L'Amande*, an intimate account of a young Arab girl's sexual awakening.

THE SWINGING 1760s

Welcome to the libidinous 18th century. Here, ladies and gentlemen, we have a short-lived golden age of sexual permissiveness, like no other time in British history. Travel and trade had opened up and London was the hub of the new Empire, bringing new prosperity and shifts in the social order which made way for a heady array of sexual experimentation. A time of randy libertines, flighty courtesans, and Molly houses offering the services of young foppish men who would make Julian Clary look like Vinnie Jones.

Folks from all walks of life indulged in such new-found pleasures as foot fetishism, flagellation, necrophilia, lesbianism, homosexuality, cross-dressing; and spawned secret sex societies such as the Hell Fire Club.

Even in such free-and-easy times, sodomy and bestiality were hanging offences. And fears of the pox did allow that socially discriminatory law, the Disorderly Houses Act, to be put on the statute books in 1751 – and which was to remain in place until just a few years ago! Generally though, any laws set down by puritanical killjoys had a hard time catching up with the breathtaking pace of change and riotous abandon.

It was not until the reign of Queen Victoria (1810-1901) that the full force of moral laws poured down to quench the fires of sexual liberation from that previous era – Victorian values whose hypocritical attitudes were to blight ordinary people's sexual freedom until the 1960s.

Bad Moon Rising: 'Taking your trousers off upside-down at 600 miles an hour can be extremely hazardous,' explained a Pentagon spokesman, in relation to the dramatic demise of a three-man US Airforce crew in a 'mooning' incident at 20,000 feet. A shocked airborne eyewitness explained, 'We were flying along when suddenly they came alongside us with their asses in the window. They were laughing and squashing their bottoms against the perspex, but then they lost control.' Tragically, before the plane went into a tailspin and crashed, the last words heard by flight controllers were, 'Nice ass, Brad!'

In the meantime, in Britain, a Chelmsford student was killed after stepping onto a busy road and mooning to an oncoming car which, if anything, just goes to prove that no matter what we British do as a nation, the Americans do it bigger and better, and with infinitely more pizzazz.

These familiar circle symbols were orginally given to the Roman deities. Mars, the god of war, represented masculinity; and the epitome of femininity was Venus (Aphrodite), the goddess of love and beauty. However, these ancient symbols only came into popular usage as recently as the 1970s.

While **Cupid** is portrayed nowadays as a cute little cherub sporting a bow and arrow, back in the days of the ancient Greeks – when pederasty was perfectly acceptable – he was a handsome naked adolescent male who embodied sexual love; after all, he was the son of Venus and Mercury. Of course, the Victorians put a stop to all that funny stuff and kitted out Cupid in that nappy-like loincloth we know today.

A BUFFER'S GUIDE TO
EROTIC ART

Pre-historic and early imagery or representations of sex had more to do with the symbolism of fertility and religion than giving the viewer the hots; there was rarely much erotic intent even in the case of the more developed Greek and Roman art – more a straightforward portrayal of the saucy tempora and mores. 10th century Indian temple sculptures as found at Khajuraho were the exception – these are full of erotic feeling or *rasa*, in Sanskrit.

Nothing much happens until the late Renaissance, with its re-interpretation of Classical art. Bronzino's *Venus, Cupid, Folly and Time* in London's National Gallery is a typical case of classical mythology supplying the excuse for lots of flesh, and the image of Cupid copping a feel of Venus' naked boobs. Most of the great painters and sculptors of the time were quite comfortable with scenes of mythological bestiality that would make today's moral guardians (and possibly the animal rights Gestapo) deeply uncomfortable, such as *Leda and the Swan, Pan and the Goat, Europa and the Bull* and so on.

In the 18th and 19th centuries, the nude became more eroticised but conversely society became more strait-laced and as so often, erotic art was driven underground. In Japan, erotic art in the shape of coloured prints flourished with artists such as Utamaro and Hokusai. These, in turn, were seen by artists like Gustave Courbet, who painted the notorious *Origin of the World* – a close-up of a gloriously hirsute female pudendum – in the 1860s. Courbet was able to sell explicit paintings to private customers, but then had no more chance of having it displayed in a national museum (as it now is) than a snowball's in hell.

This repressive atmosphere prevailed until the 1970s when both sexually explicit art and photography became more accepted and individual artists could be shown without risk of prosecution. Even so, it was not until 1985 that the first ever exhibition of erotic art in the UK was held at the Maclean Gallery in London.

Arse for Art's Sake?

At 4am on a bracing morning in July 2005, American photographer, Spencer Tunick, assembled 1,700 people in Newcastle – and persuaded them all to strip off. These brave folk had agreed to get their kit off and be herded together, in the name of art. Tunick arranges these masses of naked bodies to carpet urban landscapes and then photographs the results.

Back in 2003, he worked with smaller numbers in Selfridges store in London's Oxford Street, and on the South Bank. He has also photographed groups of 2,500 nudes in Montreal; 4,000 in Chile; 4,500 in Melbourne and 7,000 in Barcelona.

It seems there's no shortage of volunteers for these events. And Tunick has encountered no local opposition, except in New York where he was arrested several times and battled with the mayor's office for permission to photograph naked people on the city's streets, until the Supreme Court ruled that his work was protected by the American constitution.

HELLO DOLLY

If a Barbie doll was scaled up to human size, she'd be a remarkably pneumatic 39-23-33. Which may have something to do with the fact that Barbie was actually modelled on a curvy German doll with a questionable reputation, named Lilli.

Luscious Lilli was originally a busty blonde hooker, the star of a risqué cartoon strip which appeared in the *Bild-Zeitung* newspaper during the Fifties and early Sixties. And when large-breasted Lilli dolls were subsequently manufactured in Hamburg, they were originally sold in sex shops and tobacconists for the amusement of adults.

But much as the Teutonic Tit-Goddess might seem an unlikely role model for Barbie, according to the book *Forever Barbie: The Unauthorised Biography*, the original Barbie prototypes were cast from the very same mould as Lilli herself. There were alterations, of course: in contrast to her German sister, Barbie's nipples were conspicuous only by their absence. And whereas Lilli's revealing costumes made her 'the star of every bar', Barbie's wardrobe was toned down a tad.

Nevertheless, when Barbie first hit the US toy market in 1959, many parents were reluctant to buy such a 'fully sexualised woman' for their daughters and the Sears mail order company initially refused the doll in its catalogue. But Barbie instantly became a hit with young girls, and over a billion have now been sold worldwide making her one of the most successful toys ever.

Still, those T-shirts which proclaim BARBIE IS A SLUT may be closer to the truth than toy manufacturers Mattel might like to admit.

NAMES OF THE GAME

Could these be the most preposterous porn star names ever? You decide.

Tyra Misoux	Norma Stitz
April Flowers	Flick Shagwell
Olivia O'Lovely	Jewel De'Nyle
Arnold Schwartzenpecker	Seymour Butts
Johnny Depth	Ben Dover
Rubee Tuesday	Dale Da Bone
Brandon Iron	Stella Virgin
Choky Ice	Candy Apples
Maya Gold	Vince Voyeur
Jenny Love-Itt	Alyssa Allure
Puma Black	Erik Everhard
Lucy Love	Holli Woods
Tommy Gunn	Kimberly Kummings

You, too, can make up your own hardcore moniker by simply combining the name of your first pet with that of your mother's maiden name. Here are a few we came up with in the office at random:

Rex Quirk, Smokey Goulding, Lassie Finlayson, Trigger Burton, Twinkle Kitto, Lulu Dottin, Chum Wynn and Ginger Del Mar

WEIRD WORLD OF SEX #2

Weapons of Mass Seduction: According to recently declassified documents, a US airforce research team in the 1990s recommended the development of chemical weapons, made up of aphrodisiacs. The idea, devised by devious boffins in white coats, was that they would make enemy soldiers horny for one another! Not only would this divert the enemy troops from defending their position, but the guy-on-guy action would exact a heavy toll on the foe's morale – particularly against Muslim fighters. Other dastardly wheezes included directing plumes of faecal gas towards enemy lines. Phew!

EROTIC FANTASY

Everyone has sexual fantasies, whether they are elaborate lusty scenarios or fleeting erotic daydreams. Over the past 10 years, Desire magazine has published over 400 sex fantasies, written equally by female and male readers. And in the main, these were not penned by professional writers; rather, they were by individuals expressing their sexual imagination, exploring the spectrum from the seductive and sensual to the darker edges

MALE FANTASIES

- being dominated by a strict mistress
- invited to join in a threesome with another couple
- having impromptu sex with woman after a chance encounter
- dressing up as a woman
- having sex with a cross-dressing male
- having sex with two women
- having a bisexual experience with another man (often as part of a couple)
- being anally penetrated by a woman with a strap-on/dildo
- having total control over a female slave
- secretly watching partner having sex
- being humiliated while forced to watch female partner having sex with one or more men
- having sex with a decidedly younger/older woman
- sex with a familiar person (neighbour, in-law, colleague)
- doing with another something their partner is unwilling to do

EROTIC FANTASY

of the 'forbidden'. Published fantasies made liberal use of a wide variety of ingredients from oral sex and sex toys, through anal sex, fisting and watersports, to bondage and corporal punishment.

So, what are the most popular sex fantasy themes? We've compiled a Top Thirty list of scenarios, in no particular order.

FEMALE FANTASIES

- seduced by stranger into having impromptu sex
- having sex with partner and another couple
- having a bisexual experience with another woman (often as part of a couple)
- compelled to have sex with one or more males, initially against her will
- submitting to a dominant master
- being pampered, in preparation for sex
- restrained and blindfolded, then forced to have sex with two or more anonymous men, or their identity not revealed until later
- having sex with one or more men, while others watch
- using/abusing male for her satisfaction alone
- dressing up for sex
- secretly watching others having sex
- having sex with a younger male
- being centre of attention in an orgy, dogging, etc.
- using underlings/tradesmen for sexual gratification
- role-play with partner (hooker, stranger, call girl)
- indulging in an act they would not dare do in real life

EMISSION IMPOSSIBLE?

In 1981 an article entitled 'Just How the Sexes Differ' appeared in *Newsweek*, which stated that one of the major differences was that whilst men ejaculate, women do not. But as far back as 364BC, Greek philosopher Aristotle wrote about vaginal emissions which 'did not stain the sheets', and in the 17th century, a Dutch doctor, Regnier DeGraff, discovered large ducts in the urethra through which fluid was released, sometimes in large quantities. Female ejaculation remains a source of debate, with some convinced that the fluid is simply urine, despite recent evidence to the contrary. But, if it's not urine, then what is it, where does it come from, and how does it happen?

Back in the 1950s, a physician called Ernest Grafenberg discovered a bean-shaped mass of nerve tissue located approximately 2-3 inches inside the vagina.

He loved it so much, he modestly named it the G-spot, after himself. Grafenberg also discovered that stimulation of the G-spot could lead to 'large quantities of a clear, transparent fluid [being] expelled not from the vulva, but out of the urethra in gushes'.

The fluid released in female ejaculation is not urine as once commonly thought. It contains levels of glucose and an enzyme, similar to the prostate fluid released in male orgasm (without the sperm, of course). Female ejaculate comes from the para-urethral gland located in the urethral sponge (which makes up part of the G-spot). The fluid builds up during sexual arousal and is released through 32 tiny ducts into the urethra at the point of orgasm. The amount of ejaculate released by the para-urethral gland is reported to vary from a couple of drops to two cups (that's a big wet patch).

MERKIN WHOOPEE!

The pubic wig, or merkin as it was initially known, made its debut in the 1500s. Pubic hair was often shaved as a cure for syphilis, so the wealthy replaced it with wigs. It also went some way to conceal those nasty sores and pustules. Alternatively, doctors would treat the syphilitic with mercury, which caused baldness. More wigs, matron! And in days of old, one of the ways people dealt with lice was to shave off all their body hair, including the pubes. Pubic wigs caught on slowly, starting among the kinkier set, but eventually becoming halfway respectable, and fairly widely used.

Fortunately, the merkin is no longer much needed for its original function. In its more savoury contemporary role, it is now mostly used as an erotic fashion accessory. Merkins are woven from nylon or human hair onto a transparent mesh; this is then applied to the pre-shaved pubic area with spirit gum or attached to a transparent G-string. The merkin can impart a certain jaunty spring in the step, as it is worn so close to the sex organs.

Other uses for a merkin

Merkins are popular today with drag queens as they can instantly transform a cock into a pussy.

In a country of mainly dark-haired people, a prostitute may wear a blonde merkin to be unusual and so more desirable, though you can't help but wonder, would it fool anybody?

One crafty use of the merkin is to allow exotic dancers to comply with local laws prohibiting full nudity. They wear what amounts to a flesh-coloured G-string merkin, appearing to the patrons of the establishment to disrobe entirely without actually doing so.

They can be custom-made to any design: merkins have included heart-shaped pink wigs, or red, white and blue targets. What better way to demonstrate to your lover that X marks the spot?

And when the novelty wears off, a merkin makes a very acceptable cat toy.

SEX JAPANESE-STYLE

Japan is characterised on the one hand by elaborate manners and rigid social structures, and on the other by the kind of carnal extremes which have earned it the reputation as 'the most perverted country on earth'.

In September 1993, vending machines appeared in a Tokyo red-light district offering for sale knickers 'guaranteed to have been worn by a Japanese schoolgirl'. Though these machines were officially outlawed, sightings of them continue to be reported by gobsmacked tourists. But despite the machines having all but disappeared, the trade in used schoolgirl panties (and uniforms) continues unabated at sex shops. Typically, on her way home from school, a schoolgirl may earn a little pocket money by dropping her knickers off at a local erotic emporium. There they will be sealed for freshness in a plastic bag and offered for sale.

Prostitution is technically illegal in Japan, but nevertheless red-light districts flourish like nowhere else, offering an mind-boggling array of highly inventive erotic experiences. For example, in the notorious Shinjuku area of Tokyo, a man can pay to 'molest' a female traveller on a mock-up train carriage; ogle up the skirts of knickerless bar girls (courtesy of mirrored floors); or pop his pecker through a hole in the wall to be attended to in one of the many 'hand job salons'.

Though it has long been common to see commuters reading violent sadomasochistic comic books such as *Ultra Gash Inferno* on tube trains, the depiction of pubic hair remained illegal until 1991.

In the flourishing market for Japanese bestiality movies, young labrador retriever puppies are paid twice as much as their female co-stars. The mutts are known as 'butter dogs' on account of the fact that they are coaxed into performing with the aid of butter applied to their sex partner's labia. And the reason they command fees as high as 200,000 yen per movie is because they are highly-trained animals, covertly 'borrowed' from canine talent agencies which normally supply mainstream film and TV production companies.

In Japan, rope bondage (*shibari*) is a highly complex art form. During the Japanese middle ages, rope bondage was used to restrain prisoners, but during the De period (1600–1868), it developed into an aesthetic erotic art. Then, in the 1960s, numerous bondage performance clubs sprang up which featured acknowledged rope masters at work, tying up women and suspending them from elaborate pulley systems.

Nowadays *shibari* is more of an underground erotic pursuit, nevertheless with a dedicated following. Knotty but nice...

It is illegal in Japan to manufacture any objects which look like the penis – hence vibrators are invariably shaped like rabbits, cats, dolphins and other animals.

It is estimated that there are nearly 40,000 *rabu hoteru* (love hotels) throughout Japan, with 4,000 in Tokyo alone. These are not brothels, but rather premises which are specifically designed for people to have sex in.

Sure, businessmen may book in with prostitutes or even with their secretaries; but in a country where most young adults live with their parents until they marry, they're hugely popular with courting couples.

Often outlandishly decorated with kitschy, themed rooms, love hotels come equipped with everything from vibrating beds to sunken baths, SM equipment and a selection of porno DVDs. Many rooms even have vending machines selling sex toys.

Every day, around one million couples check in to a love hotel.

It must have come as quite a shock to the pupils of Mr **Ron Jeremy** when their school teacher handed in his cap and gown and went on to become the world's biggest porn star. Born into a high-acheiving family, he originally entertained the notion of leaving teaching behind to become a regular thespian. Then in 1978 a girlfriend submitted a picture of him to *Playgirl* magazine for the 'Boy Next Door' feature and a super stud was born. Between then and now he's starred in over 1700 hardcore films, and has also found time to direct another 250!

The cocksman they now call The Hedgehog has become ubiquitous, to the point that *AVN (Adult Video News)* named him the Top Porn Star of All Time. To put that into perspective, Jenna Jameson was at number two, and John Holmes at number three. The secret of his broad appeal seems to be largely due to the fact that his body (short, fat and hairy describes him fairly well) and persona are that of a regular Joe – although his impressive ten-inch penis doesn't hinder his fame either. An XXX industry joke is that when casting for porno movies, female stars are routinely asked: 'Will you do anal? Double penetration? Ron Jeremy?'

The adult industry loves him for his down-to-earth approach to his trade. No prima donna antics: and he's refreshingly realistic about the reasons for the large discrepancy in men and women's pay for porn, observing, 'Men are more willing; there are fewer women who would want to do it. Guys would do it for the sex alone.' To complete his 'living legend' status, an accaimed film has been made about him, *Porn Star: The Legend of Ron Jeremy*. Even the mainstream media has taken him to their hearts as the acceptable face of XXX, to the extent that he starred in reality TV series, *The Farm*.

■ **Ron Jeremy has a nifty technique that probably makes him the envy of quite a few men. He can suck his own dick, and claims he discovered the pleasures of auto-fellation while tying his shoelaces, aged 14.**

TWENTY-SEVEN BRIDES FOR ONE BROTHER

Brigham Young of the Mormons had 27 wives – and, of course, 27 mothers-in-law! Though Mormon founder Joseph Smith had at least 30 wives, a fact he kept a secret from his first wife, Emma. Oddly, she later married Brigham Young in open polygamy. Guess she was a sharing kind of a gal. The Mormons can no longer practise polygamy legally in the USA.

Africa's last absolute monarch, 37-year-old King Mswati III of Swaziland, is about to take his 13th bride. He selects his young bride from 50,000 virgins, all over the age of 13, who dance bare-breasted before him. A little spoilt for choice... Though he's got a lot of catching up to do, as his late father, King Sobuza II, is said to have married 112 women and sired 600 children.

The practice of polygamy really is as old as the hills: according to the *Old Testament*, King Solomon had seven hundred wives – oh, and three hundred concubines.

Islam, allows a man to have up to four wives, though they should all have their own property, assets and dowry, and in some Muslim countries it is illegal for a man to have multiple wives if he cannot take care of them financially. For women, however, Islam insists they should be content with just one husband at a time.

Generally though, we would hazard a guess that having just one spouse at a time is all that most people can cope with. Just ask any divorce lawyer.

COMING ATTRACTIONS

The Big O. Right, we're not talking the residual term of a truncated infinite series here, just in case you're a mathematician. Or even the late Roy Orbison. We're talking about that 1960s expression for coming, for getting your John O'Groats, for an orgasm.

Back then, suddenly everyone wanted to have as many as possible and if your life lacked the Big O, well, it was definitely lacking. Just as its contemporary, the Big Mac, became the hero of fast food, so the Big O, promoted by 60s and 70s sex gurus, became the nirvana of sexual intercourse.

So what actually happens when you have an orgasm? We could just tell you that it's 'a super feeling' – its sobriquet in a well-known private girls' school, we hear – but no, we're serious fact-mongers, so... (but let's just get one out of the way first: both male and female transsexuals enjoy perfectly decent orgasms, although the female-to-male variety can't ejaculate).

Male orgasms go like this. After prolonged stimulation, usually of the penis, three separate parts of the body start things moving with quick, rhythmic contractions – the prostrate, the urethra and the muscles at the base of the penis. These contractions blast stored semen out of the hole in the top of the penis (meatus) for a period of three to ten seconds. The feelings experienced by the orgasmic one during this event are pretty fine; but apparently a finger or vibrating dildo up the bum can even enhance them if it stimulates the prostrate gland.

There are other, more violent, stimuli that might provoke a bitchin' good ejaculation, such as slow strangulation or hanging, but these are, on the whole, best discounted. Post orgasm, depending on age, most men need a recovery period of an hour to half a day during which their parts are 'refractory', or not able to respond to stimulus.

Female orgasms occur for similar reasons, ie sexual stimulation, but they are more complex and mysterious and fraught with scientific controversy. The interior of the vagina becomes wet, the clitoris and labia enlarge, the body sometimes blushes a pretty pink, the clitoris dives for cover under its hood, the labia minora become darker. Then finally, just prior to contractions, the vagina decreases in size by 30 per cent, which, of course, is highly considerate of it if it happens to be entertaining a penis at the time.

A full orgasm is deemed to be when the womb, the vagina and the pelvic muscles all rhythmically contract at the same time; while the cervix convulses and dips to draw any semen present into the uterus.

Unlike men, women don't have a refractory period and can sail merrily on to the next orgasm. And the next. And the next...

The bad news for girls is that a third of women can't achieve orgasm during intercourse. Most women often need additional stimulation, such as clitoral stimulation in order to orgasm.

When climaxing, some women ejaculate fluid, thought to be from Skene's glands located on the upper wall of the vagina.

> **Note:**
> A real orgasm burns 112 calories; a faked orgasm burns 515.

COMING ATTRACTIONS

HOW OLD IS OLD ENOUGH?

The legal age of consent for heterosexual sex

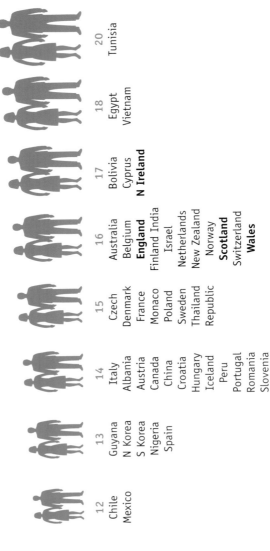

12	13	14	15	16	17	18	20
Chile	Guyana	Italy	Czech	Australia	Bolivia	Egypt	Tunisia
Mexico	N Korea	Albania	Denmark	Belgium	Cyprus	Vietnam	
	S Korea	Austria	France	**England**	**N Ireland**		
	Nigeria	Canada	Monaco	Finland India			
	Spain	China	Poland	Israel			
		Croatia	Sweden	Netherlands			
		Hungary	Thailand	New Zealand			
		Iceland	Republic	Norway			
		Peru		**Scotland**			
		Portugal		Switzerland			
		Romania		**Wales**			
		Slovenia					

✳ In the USA, ages 16–18, varying from state to state.

www.ageofconsent.com

50 | CARNAL KNOWLEDGE

COCK ROCK

There are any number of obscure bands known by outrageously sexual names, but also a good number of better-known ones. While names such as **The Slits**, **The Muffs**, **Hole** and **Throbbing Gristle** need no explanation, the source of others may be a little less obvious. For example, both **10cc** and the **Lovin' Spoonful** were christened in honour of the average amount of sperm issued upon ejaculation. And while it has been suggested that **Pearl Jam** is another spunky name, some maintain that the sticky sobriquet actually refers to the lead singer's granny, Pearl, who made great jam…

Steely Dan meanwhile, were named after a metal dildo which featured in a William Burroughs novel, while **Joy Division** references a group of female concentration camp prisoners who were forced to service Nazi officers, in the novel *The House of Dolls* by Karol Cetinsky. Similarly, the **Velvet Underground** lifted their name from a Sixties book exposing sensationalised exploits of fetishists and kinksters. Don Van Vliet was apparently inspired to call himself **Captain Beefheart** in honour of a dodgy uncle whose party trick was to squeeze his penis until the head turned purple and exclaim it looked like 'a big ole beef heart'. And Seventies band **Three Dog Night** were seemingly inspired by the Eskimo custom of sleeping with three dogs on extremely cold nights.

Punk bands **The Buzzcocks** and **The Vibrators** clearly shared a common source of inspiration. Shane McGowan was once a member of the **Nipple Erectors** and Simple Minds started out as **Johnny and the Self Abusers**. Also on the 'self-abuse' theme, the name of American hardcore outfit, **Circle Jerks**, refers to a form of group masturbation. And while macho metallers **AC/DC** claim to have been naively unaware of any bisexual connotations pertaining to their name, not so the brilliantly named 'queercore' rockers, **Pansy Division**. Just avoid front row seats if you're planning to see a gig by new Norwegian band, **The Cum Shots**.

THE HOT PARADE

This was the recent American critics' choice of the top twenty adult movies of all time. No surprise, then, that the selection overlooks classic European movies such as *Sensations* and *Caligula* and, um... can't think of any more!

Night Trips 1989
(Dir: Andrew Blake)
Tori Welles, Porsche
Lynn, Peter North

Nothing to Hide 1983
(Anthony Spinelli)
John Leslie, Richard
Pacheco, Chelsea
Manchester

Latex/ Shock 1995
(Michael Ninn)
Tyffany Million, Sunset
Thomas, Jon Dough

Behind the Green Door
1972
(Jim & Artie Mitchell)
Marilyn Chambers

Justine:
Nothing to Hide 2 1993
(Paul Thomas)
Roxanne Blaze, Mike
Horner

Scoundrels 1983
(Cecil Howard)
Lisa Be, Chelsea
Manchester, Ron Jeremy

Bobby Sox 1996
(Paul Thomas)
Nikki Tyler, Shanna
McCullough, Steven St
Croix

Buttman's European
Vacation 1991
(John Stagliano)
Rocco Siffredi, Zara
Whites, Sunny McCay

Opening of Misty
Beethoven 1975
(Henry Paris)
Gloria Leonard,
Constance Money,
Jamie Gillis

Dog Walker 1994
(John Leslie)
Krysti Lynn, Christina
Angel, Steven St Croix

Devil in Miss Jones
3 & 4 1986
(Gregory Dark)
Vanessa Del Rio, Amber
Lynn, Jack Baker

Insatiable 1980
(Godfrey Daniels)
Marilyn Chambers,
Jessie St James,
John Holmes

Drop Sex 1997
(John Leslie)
Kimberly Jade,
Mikki Malone,
Valentino

Debbie Does
Dallas 1982
(Gerard Damiano)
Bambi Woods, R Bolla

Café Flesh 1982
(Rinse Dream)
Pia Snow, Kevin James

Sex World
1978
(Anthony Spinelli)
Annette Haven, John
Leslie, Leslie Bovee

New Wave Hookers
1985
(Gregory Dark)
Ginger Lynn, Kristara
Barrington, Jack Baker

The Devil in Miss Jones
1972
(Gerard Damiano)
Georgina Spelvin,
Harry Reems

Face Dance 1 & 2
1992
(John Stagliano)
Tyffany Million, Tiffany
Mynx, Rocco Siffredi

Bad Wives
1997
(Paul Thomas)
Dyanna Lauren, Missy,
Stephanie Swift,
Steven St Croix

**check www.avn.com
for a full list of the
101 greatest XXX
films ever**

Shit a brick! **The American Journal of Forensic Medicine & Pathology** *records the case of a young gay man who turned up at at his local hospital complaining of a severe pain in the arse. Doctors were dumbfounded when a digital examination of the rectum revealed the presence of a large, hard stony mass - later identified as a lump of concrete. When pressed for an explanation, the man confirmed that some hours earlier he had been making whoopee with his partner and, after mixing a batch of concrete (as one does) he lay on his back with his legs against the wall, while his boyfriend poured the mixture through a funnel into his rectum, before finally inserting a ping-pong ball to act as a plug. Later diagnosed as an experienced klismaphiliac (enema enthusiast to you and me), the man had apparently fallen asleep.*

The patient was kept in hospital overnight where, under anaesthesia, doctors delivered without complications a perfect 11b 2oz concrete cast of the man's rectum and lower intestine.

DAVID'S PIZZLE PUZZLE

Ever since Michelangelo completed his 14-feet-high statue of David back in 1504, it has been admired as a remarkably accurate representation of the perfect male form. Yet for Italians and visitors to Florence, the rather modest size of David's tackle has been a constant source of amusement. So why did the sculptor not make him better endowed?

Now two doctors believe they have come up with an explanation, having examined the marble figure more closely when it was cleaned in 2004.

Michelangelo was portraying David as he challenged the giant Goliath and, in the face of extreme danger, David's dick simply shrivelled. After all, the figure's other anatomical details suggest fear, tension, aggression and concentration: wide-open eyes, furrowed brow and flared nostrils. Stress and fear cause adrenaline to be released which restricts the flow of blood and so another marked effect would be a dramatic contraction of the genitals.

Well, that clears one little mystery, then. But since David was Jewish, why did Michelangelo not sculpt him as circumcised?

To commemorate the 3,000th anniversary of David's conquest of Jerusalem, the city of Florence presented Jerusalem with a replica of Michelangelo's statue of David.

But it seems Jerusalem's religious leaders considered the nude figure to be so pornographic that Florence commissioned a second statue as a replacement – this time fully clothed.

D-I-Y

Both men and women are more likely to experience their first orgasm through masturbation. According to most surveys, over 90 per cent of men and women admit to masturbating – and the remainder are liars. After all, as Woody Allen advised, 'Don't knock it, it's sex with someone you love.'

Do the Zombie Shuffle
If you lie on one arm for some time until it goes completely numb, then wank with that hand, it feels like someone else is doing it to you!

Flakes, Nuts and Crackers: The Anti-masturbation Crusade

Next time you're tucking into breakfast with a bowl of Kellogg's Corn Flakes or Post Grape Nuts or some Graham crackers, you might like to know that the Americans who gave their names to these snacks were killjoy zealots who believed that excessive masturbation and sexual activity were seriously detrimental to your health!

John H Kellogg, CW Post and Sylvester Graham believed masturbation was self-pollution. However, for Graham this was not a moral issue, but one of health and longevity. He believed masturbation caused shyness, disregard for hygiene, and filled the body with disease, and caused acne (the 'ulcerous sores' and 'foetid pus' could lead to death).

Following Graham, Post and Kellogg claimed a vegetarian diet high in whole grains would curb sexual hunger. Pioneering cold cereal breakfasts in the Kellogg Sanatorium, a hospital for the promotion of good health through diet, exercise, enemas and the suppression of sexual desire, Kellogg and Post fed their patients with corn flakes, shredded wheat, and Graham's eponymous crackers. WK Kellogg, Dr Kellogg's entrepreneurial brother, was less interested in crusading against masturbation and saw a potential gold mine in cold cereals. How right he was.

NUDE AWAKENING

These are the most popular destinations abroad for getting all your kit off, according to H&E Naturist *magazine (www.henaturist.co.uk) which represents nudists across the spectrum.*

Cap d'Agde Situated in the Languedoc region of France, the world's largest naturist resort can trace its history back to the 1950s. Originally a camping and caravanning site, it soon grew into Europe's first naturist town, complete with supermarkets, restaurants, banks and shops.

Vera Playa While not quite on the same scale as Cap d'Agde, this Spanish resort embraces the same naturist community spirit. There are no barriers between the naturist zone (some 2,000 properties – all privately-owned – a hotel and a campsite) and the outside world which makes for a very laid-back atmosphere.

Koversada First set up in 1961, Koversada is Croatia's oldest naturist resort. Originally sited on the island of Koversada, the resort soon spread to the Istrian peninsula and can now accommodate 820 people in terraced pavilions, plus a further 5,000 campers and caravanners.

A favourite with couples and families alike.

Caliente There are numerous naturist resorts in Florida, USA, but probably the newest and most luxurious of these is Caliente. This self-contained village is clothing-optional rather than strictly naturist, but most people stay nude from morning to night to enjoy the lavish facilities, lush gardens and relaxing spa.

Hedonism II & Hedonism III Seen by many as being more nudist than naturist, Jamaica's two Hedonism resorts are targeted at 'self-indulgent' adults: strictly no children allowed. Renowned for promoting a liberal lifestyle and uninhibited party atmosphere, at Hedo anything and everything goes.

Incidentally, you can bathe naked on any beach in New Zealand, just so long as no-one complains.

Dare to be Bare

Vincent Bethell was the first man to stand naked in an English court, and has been prosecuted countless times for public nudity offences. And even while on remand for five months in Brixton prison, he refused to wear any clothes.

Stephen Gough, walked from Land's End to John O'Groats, in only his hiking boots. The naked rambler was arrested over a dozen times and served two prison sentences. Undeterred, he set off in the summer of 2005 to retread his steps, only this time in the company of a naked girlfriend. And remarkably, they got all the way to Shropshire before being arrested. But it seems the enlightened locals came out in their defence, saying they would have no objection to encountering a nude rambler.

The top hot spots for acquiring an all-over suntan in England and Wales

Morfa Dyffryn, Gwynedd
A choice destination for naturists since the 1930s, this expansive golden beach, located in Snowdonia National Park, was the first official nudist beach in Wales.

Studland, Dorset
The UK's best-known beach for baring all. Situated near Swanage, this sandy beach backed by dunes, and run by the National Trust, is popular for its laid-back European style.

Slapton Sands, Devon
Secluded fine-shingle beach, near Dartmouth, with great views and a easy-going atmosphere, a favourite amongst nudists for years.

Holkham, Norfolk
The naturist section is part of a vast unspoilt stretch of beach (pictured), surrounded by a nature reserve, on the northern coast of East Anglia.

THE TEEN STARLET WHO NEARLY SANK THE XXX BIZ

Though she was one of hardcore's hottest young starlets, **Traci Lords** is remembered with little affection by most within the American jizz biz. She almost single-handedly brought the entire industry crashing to its knees in the mid-eighties, when the US federal authorities got wind of the fact that all bar one of her 107 hardcore films were made when she was underage. In the United States you have to be eighteen or over to appear in porno, and Traci was sweet fifteen when she made her first movie.

The resultant court case revealed that Traci (real name, Nora Louise Kuzma) had used fake ID, which stated she was 22 years old, to break into the adult industry. In fact, the Justice Department had to drop all charges against the distributor of Lords' movies when it was revealed that she had used the same ID to dupe the government into issuing her with an adult passport – so allowing her visit Japan to shoot *Traci Takes Tokyo*!

Nevertheless, the Traci Lords affair proved costly to the American porn industry, both in terms of money and adverse publicity; the latter being especially damaging at a time when the Reaganite authorities were intent on wiping out the skin trade altogether. Millions of dollars were lost as the industry was obliged to remove from the shelves and destroy all videos and magazine pictorials featuring the teen vixen. And the episode culminated in the passing of a new law requiring adult producers to maintain documents proving the identity and legal age of all their models.

Though now officially classified as 'child porn' in the States, Lords' hardcore movies remain legally available in much of Europe where the minimum legal age for working in porn is sixteen. Traci has subsequently enjoyed a moderately successful career as a mainstream actress and singer but her recent autobiography *Underneath it All* was criticised for glossing over her cream queen past.

AND THE BANNED PLAYED ON

These songs were banned at one time or another on radio or TV. Here's why...

Je T'Aime Pas – Jane Birkin & Serge Gainsbourg (1969)
In which Lothario Serge interspersed Jane's orgasmic groans with musings on the joy of going *'entre tes reins'* or between your kidneys (up the arse, allegedly).

French Kiss – Lil Louis (1989)
Banned for 'heavy breathing'.

I Can't Control Myself – The Troggs (1966)
The sound that Reg Presley makes at the end of the song was said to sound like someone climaxing.

Relax – Frankie Goes To Hollywood (1983)
Frankie said 'Relax' but the BBC balked at the suggestive lyrics: 'Relax, don't do it / When you want to go to it / Relax, don't do it / When you want to come.' It was all too much for DJ Mike Read, who primly objected to the 'overtly obscene lyrical content'.

Honky Tonk Angel – Cliff Richard (1972)
This was a self-imposed ban, when Sir Cliff discovered that a honky tonk angel was, in fact, a hooker!

Let's Spend The Night Together – The Rolling Stones (1967)
Apparently, it 'promoted promiscuity'.

Wet Dream – Max Romeo (1969)
The BBC wouldn't buy the story that this was an innocent song about his bedroom ceiling!

Open Your Box – Yoko Ono Plastic Ono Band (1970)
Banned for containing the lyric 'Open your legs'.

BAD GIRLS

Cleopatra (69-30BC), the last pharaoh of Egypt, married her younger brother Ptolemy when he was 12 (they did that sort of thing in Egypt back then). When he drowned in the Nile, she married an even younger brother, aged 11, also called Ptolemy. She was smuggled into Julius Caesar's palace rolled up in a rug, and then seduced him. Though no oil painting, Cleo was a brilliant seductress: later she added Mark Anthony to her list by visiting him on a barge with silver oars, purple sails, and a golden stern and crewed by maids dressed as sea nymphs. Cleopatra dressed as Venus, seated on a golden dais and fanned by boys wearing only Cupid's wings. Won over by this massive display of vulgarity, or possibly by her reputation for being a record-breaking fellatrice*, he too fell to her charms.

She is remembered by a Shakespearean play, a spuriously named obelisk, an epic Hollywood movie starring Liz Taylor, an epic hardcore movie and a vibrator set called 'Cleopatra's Treasures'.
*The Greeks called her Merichane, the wide-mouthed one, following an account of her having fellated 100 Roman noblemen – in one night.

Messalina

Of all the bad girls in history, Messalina, left, (23-48AD) is up there with the finalists. At 15 she became the Emperor Claudius' third wife and bore him an heir. A great party animal, this nymphomaniac, sulky teen had no problems with using her body for ruthless political ends. She took many lovers and rather unpleasantly duped Claudius into executing them if the affair went sour.

She once challenged the famous Roman whore Scylla to an all-night shagging contest. Scylla dropped out at daybreak but Messalina was still going strong by mid-morning. Her husband had her executed for plotting his death and for secretly marrying Silius, a potential rival.

Elizabeth Bathory

Countess Elizabeth Bathory-Nadasdy (1560-1614), a Magyar royal, was married off at the age of 15 to a play-away soldier who left this proto Goth babe much to her own devices in his Transylvanian castle; these included flaying her victims' softer parts with a particularly vicious silver-clawed whip. When hubby was stabbed to death by a peevish Bucharest tart, Elizabeth sought a lover; no longer in the first flush of youth she found the going tough.

When she struck her maid and was splashed accidentally by this young virgin's blood, her skin appeared to rejuvenate itself. The delighted Countess set about kidnapping local virgins wholesale, tying them by their feet from the bathroom rafters and then cutting their throats to bathe in and drink their blood. Convinced that she was worth it, she dispatched more than 600 in this way, peasants and wellborn alike. The authorities finally caught up with her and curtailed her virgin-harvesting activities by having her walled up in a tiny room.

Half the world has one and half the world likes to have one as much as possible. Men are very protective when it comes to their most treasured possession. The majority spend many an anxious hour checking it is there, checking again to be sure and generally worrying about size, shape, whether it will let them down, and how they measure up to other men. Relax, here are some of the facts to reassure you that your member is perfectly normal (just don't compare yourself to the blue whale).

The average length of a human penis when not erect is 3.5 inches. The average length of a human penis when erect is 5.87 inches.

When Alfred Kinsey conducted a study of penis size in the 1940s, he found the average penis size to be 6.3 inches, which lead many men to feel that they were coming up, well, a bit short. It seems that many of Kinsey's subjects were stretching the truth somewhat. Left on their own to mark off the length of their erect member on a piece of card, most couldn't resist adding on half an inch or so.

When a more recent study was conducted with a doctor and nurse measuring 300 erect penises, the average was found to be 5.87 inches, with two-thirds of the men ranging from 5.1 to 6.2 inches, with an average circumference of 4.9 inches.

The largest human penis recorded was a whopping 13 inches long while the smallest was a measly five-eighths of an inch. The blue whale boosts the largest member in the animal kingdom at a gargantuan 11 feet and a rhinoceros penis is at least two feet long. However, human males take heart, for you are in possession of the largest and thickest penis of all the primates – an adult gorilla's penis is only about two inches long. King Dong, I think not. On the downside, a small proportion of human males suffer from a

FACTS & PHALLUSES

condition called micropenis measuring between 0.75 to 1 inch long, but on the upside, a lucky 0.3% of men are well-endowed enough to fellate themselves. I bet they don't get out much. Take heed, a man's penis shrinks not only in cold weather, but also from non-sexual excitement. So steer clear of rollercoasters if you're trying to impress a lady.

Phalloplasty is the surgical lengthening of the penis (not used often by blue whales), involving cutting the suspensory ligaments on the top of the penis allowing it to extend to a greater length. In cases where the penis is drastically smaller than normal, it can be extended using skin grafts taken from the groin. If it's girth you're looking to increase, fat can be suctioned off other areas of the body and injected into the penis. Every year, over 6,000 American males have their penises lengthened.

From the last trimester, a male foetus is capable of getting an erection and from then on it doesn't stop until old age or death, with three-quarters of 70-year-old men still able to maintain an erection.

The amount of time needed for a man to regain an erection after orgasm ranges from two minutes to two weeks depending on age, but the average man has 11 erections every day and 9 per night. With so many erections around, it's not surprising that some people suffer from *ithyphallophobia*, the fear of seeing, thinking about, or having an erect penis, while others are *medomalacuphobic* and fear losing an erection. How very careless.

■ Napoleon's penis was sold to an American urologist for $40,000. Can't believe they cut it off.
■ In 1995 in Hong Kong, a Chi Kung master called Mo Ka Wang lifted over 250 pounds two feet off the floor using only his erect penis. Give the man a pat on the back.
■ Dragonflies have shovel-shaped penises which they use to scoop out the sperm of male rivals. Maybe they just detest sloppy seconds.

NUDGE-NUDGE, WINK-WINK

Smut derives from the German word *schmutz* meaning dirt.

Horny probably derived from the cow or bull, as the bull's horn resembles the male erection. I know which I'd rather be penetrated by!

The Latin source of **carnal** is *caro*, meaning flesh. Carnal knowledge is knowledge of the flesh.

The Ancient Greeks referred to the **genitals** as *pudendum* which means shame.

Since 1900 there have been more than 1,300 slang words for **penis**. The most widely used today is **cock**. When a rooster becomes excited the wattles and comb on its neck and head fill with blood causing them to swell and expand. Just like a penis.

Clever, eh? Another popular term for the penis is **dick**. There have been several male names for the cock starting with Roger (yes, it's true), Thomas in 1811, Dick (1891), Peter (1902) and Willie (1905) – typically male names of the times.

The word **cunt** started out perfectly respectably. But by the 14th century the word had become taboo, and by the late 18th century it was considered so shocking that it appeared in Francis Grose's *Dictionary of the Vulgar Tongue* as merely 'a nasty name for a nasty thing.'

Beaver came into vogue in the 1920s, which led to the term beaver shot in the 1960s: a porno pic which focuses on… the beaver, of course.

Did you know that in ancient England, when people wanted to make babies, they had to get permission from the king and were given a placard stating 'FUCK' to assert that they could Fornicate Under Consent of the King? Well, it isn't true.

The origin of the word is difficult to trace. When compiling the *Oxford English Dictionary* (1893-97), *fuck* was taboo to the editors. The modern written forms and an earlier version *fukkit* are found from the 16th century forward, though the surname *Fucker* dates back to 1278. A 15th century Latin poem, includes a delightful use of *fuccant*. Roughly translated: 'The monks are not in heaven because they fuck the wives of Ely.'

EMPIRE OF THE CENSORS

Following 'video nasties' tabloid hysteria, the government introduced the Video Recordings Act in 1984, which states that a video sold without a certificate contravenes the law, and so the **British Board of Film Censors** was appointed to censor videos, too. Around the same time, the BBFC adopted the more fluffy moniker, British Board of Film Classification.

When explicit hardcore porn was legalised in this country in 2000, it was assigned a special 'Restricted' certificate, R18, by the BBFC, with the proviso that such material can only be purchased in licensed sex shops. In what some producers consider an additional 'tax', they have to pay around £800 (£7 per minute) to get a 2-hour movie passed for release. So there's still a fair chance that your hardcore movie has been already cut by the censors, as the BBFC's own statistics show:

	R18 films passed	% with cuts
2004	1,387	21
2003	1,405	18
2002	1,061	15
2001	651	7
2000	212	13

A couple of years ago, John 'Buttman' Staglioni's SM-flavoured hardcore epic, *Fashionistas*, was subjected to a total of 24 minutes of cuts before being granted an R18 certificate.

■ In case you ever wondered who would spend their day in a darkened room watching hours of hardcore films – in order to protect us from ourselves – the current panel of censors (sorry, examiners) include lawyers, civil servants, teachers, social workers, journalists and a doctor.

RINGS'N'THINGS

These days you're just not keeping up with the Joneses if you don't have at least one intimate part of your anatomy pierced. Piercings should not be undertaken lightly, but here are some facts and tips if you decide to go ahead.

For Him

Foreskin piercings are quick to heal, though the foreskin comfortably accommodates only one or two piercings. A series of **horizontal barbells** through the skin of the penis can create a 'ladder' up the shaft.

The **Prince Albert** is probably the most popular of all male genital piercings, in which a ball closure ring is worn through the urethra at the base of the penis head. It has the drawback that it may partially impede urination.

An **ampallang** is a horizontal piercing through the glans, which is said to have originated in Borneo where apparently women would refuse to sleep with men who didn't have one. The **apadravya** is a vertical version of the ampallang.

Love beads are not really piercings, but 'sub-skin implants', in which small beads are placed beneath the skin specifically for the added stimulation of your partner during intercourse.

For Her

The **inner labia** is probably the most popular of all the female genital piercings, usually made through the upper part of the inner labia. The **outer labia** takes longer to heal than the inner labia, due to the greater thickness of the tissue. The **clitoral hood** can be pierced

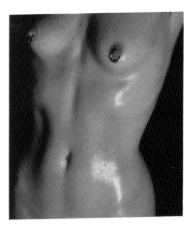

horizontally with a barbell or ring; or vertically, usually with a ring. The **clitoris** is particularly stimulating although potentially problematic, and many practitioners refuse to perform this piercing.

As its name suggests, the **Princess Albertina** is the female equivalent of the Prince Albert. A ring is placed through the urethral opening and exits a short distance below.

For Him & For Her

A **guiche** is a piercing through the ridge of skin between the back of the scrotum and anus for men, and between the back of the vagina and the anus for women.

A **nipple piercing** can heighten sensitivity for both women and men. Usually pierced horizontally, but can also be pierced vertically or diagonally. Nipple piercings for women were actually fashionable as early as the 1890s, where they were worn by hip Parisienne women. Known as **anneaux de seins** (rings of the breast), they would often be worn one in each nipple and linked together with a delicate chain.

Finally, when it comes to oral sex, the caresses of a **pierced tongue** can be fabulously stimulating.

Under Pressure: Forcing air into the rectum with a bicycle pump became a popular pastime amongst young males in Thailand in the mid-90s.

In search of the ultimate buzz, Chamchai P decided that bicycle pumps were for wimps and chose to use a compressed air hose on a service station forecourt.

Unfortunately, Chamchai succeeded only in blowing himself to little pieces, much to the astonishment of a Ms Ra who was filling up with three-star at the time. 'I thought it was a fireworks display,' she was heard to tell drop-jawed reporters.

When asked about the prevalence of 'pumping' amongst the country's youth, a police spokesman suggested that the matter had been 'blown out of all proportion'.

T&A (TITS & ASS)

The average man in the street can be forgiven for ogling tits and bums, two of the main sexual attractions that a clothed woman's body can provide. They are, barring an encounter on a nudist beach or in more intimate circumstances, the two most prominent secondary sex characteristics visible and, hey, Nature put them there to be ogled. Some anthropologists feel that female breasts, by mimicking buttocks, persuaded men to eschew the doggy position and adopt the missionary one, thereby reproducing more efficiently. Others think it's more to do with gazing into each other's eyes and thus bonding as you bonk.

A common misconception is that big breasts produce lots of milk. Wrong. The milk factory takes up very little of the breast's overall size. And talking of size, the average bra size in the UK has increased from a 34B in the 1950s to a 36C today, though whether this is accelerated evolution or better diet isn't clear. But the good news is that 'Topfree' equality movements to go topless on beaches and in parks will ensure greater freedom for girls and more ogling for boys in the near future.

And bums. The bigger the better? Not as simple as that, sadly: Hottentot tribeswomen stored so much buttock fat that early explorers would place a beer bottle and two glasses on the ledge thus formed, and in 1810, Saartjie Baartman, the 'Hottentot Venus' was cruelly displayed in Piccadilly as a sexual freak. Ironically, in the Victorian era, the bustle was to extend society ladies' derrières to similar distances.

In some primitive or Islamic cultures, bottoms, being rich in nerve endings, have been favourite targets for public punishment: they protect the genitals and spine, minimizing real injury, leave no permanent marks and induce maximum humiliation when semi-exposed for public caning. By contrast, in Western culture, spanking is now considered an important part of sexual foreplay by many couples while others may go further and indulge in serious, S&M-type caning.

If ever there were a poll to decide who was the most depraved and debauched individual of the 20th century, then French artist **Pierre Molinier** would surely be a worthy winner.

Born in 1900, even as a three-year-old he exhibited early signs of a lifelong erotic fixation with female legs, running his hands up the skirts of his mother's shocked friends, as well as of his sister Julienne. Then, following Julienne's sudden death in 1918, Molinier claimed to have become so turned on by his sister's corpse that he ejaculated across her stomach and legs. 'She took with her into death the best of me,' he commented.

Molinier moved to Bordeaux in his early twenties, where he became a fixture at the seaport's numerous brothels, eventually even setting up one of his daughters as the madame of one. In his forties and fifties, his sexual explorations grew ever more extreme. He spent two years designing a contraption which would allow him to fellate himself and then upon completion, spent fourteen days locked away in his garret living solely on a diet of his own semen. Molinier also experimented with self-sodomy.

By the late-Sixties, Molinier's notoriety ensured that a steady stream of men and women made the pilgrimage to Bordeaux to be sodomised and/or photographed by him. As well as beautiful models – such as Emmanuelle Arsan, author of the *Emmanuelle* books – Molinier's explicit and highly fetishistic photographs often featured the artist himself, naked apart from stockings and high heels. Molinier was diagnosed with prostate cancer, aged seventy-five. But rather than die a slow and lingering death, the lusty surrealist pinned a note to his door which declared, 'Being alive makes me shit, so I am now killing myself of my own free will and I'm going to have a great time doing it.' He then lay back on his bed and masturbated for the last time, putting a bullet to his brain at the point of ejaculation. Way to go, Pierre!

CONSUMED WITH LUST

Humans have always experimented with foods, drugs, lotions and potions in a quest for the ultimate elixir of love, lust and romance, and in the hope of boosting sexual vigour. And one thing is certain: they are far more likely to provide that extra oomph to those who believe that they might just work. Of course, an active, varied sex life enlivened by imaginative fantasy is a pretty potent aphrodisiac in itself. So, when used in tandem with our own natural sexual prowess, the more aphrodisiacs the merrier! Bring it on… Here are just a few of Aphrodite's little helpers.

foods

Eastern cultures have for centuries drawn on a wealth of lust-provoking recipes in such erotic manuals as *The Perfumed Garden* and *Kama Sutra,* involving hot spices like chilies, ginger and coriander. Beans, mushrooms, asparagus, eggs, toads' hearts and larks' tongues have all been imbued with erotic properties at different times. Better still if, like bananas, cucumbers or figs, they resemble certain parts of the male or female anatomy.

Most seafoods were accorded aphrodisiac status by the Romans, partially because of their association with the sea, from whence arose love goddess Venus. And when first imported from the New World, avocados, tomatoes ('love apples') and even potatoes were believed to have sexually stimulating properties, largely attributable to their exotic source and rarity.

A high sugar content ensures honey's reputation as a sweet companion to sex (check out the fridge scene in *91/2 Weeks*). It has featured in countless aphrodisiac recipes and was thought, like salt, to strengthen and lengthen the effect of love potions and spells. Barbara Cartland swears by it, though that's hardly a recommendation!

Then there's chocolate: the long list of chocolate lovers (including of course every woman in the world) includes such notables as Madame du Barry, Casanova and the Marquis de Sade: its lascivious reputation was such that the Spanish Inquisition felt compelled to outlaw it. The cocoa bean contains phenelethylamine, a mood-altering drug which lends a feeling of well-being. Little wonder the lady loves Milk Tray.

The Romans considered **oysters** an aphrodisiac partially due to its resemblance to the female genitals. Emperor Vitellis is reputed to have devoured one thousand at a sitting, but the effects of this blow-out don't appear to have been recorded. They were also a cheap source of protein for the Victorian poor!

The less romantic among us may draw the conclusion it's no coincidence that vitamins and minerals known to promote sexual health are so often plentiful in foods traditionally considered aphrodisiac. Oysters and anchovies for example are rich in phosphorous, copper and zinc and it would follow that any food which promoted good health, strength and stamina would enhance sexual desire.

drugs and pharmaceuticals

Strictly speaking, **alcohol** cannot be classified as a sexual stimulant, although by increasing blood flow and lowering inhibitions, it does cause mild arousal. But as Shakespeare wryly observed in Macbeth, and as we all know from experience, it often 'provokes the desire but it takes away the performance'. Recreational drugs such as marijuana, cocaine and amphetamines can justifiably claim to enhance sex, reduce inhibitions and delay orgasm to some extent, but they can also prove to be counterproductive or even dangerous if taken to excess. Apart from which, many of them are illegal.

Cocaine affords a feeling of mental, physical and sexual prowess, and also prolongs sex and delays orgasm. While it lowers sexual inhibitions, it can also impair performance. Applied directly to the glans or clitoris, cocaine's anaesthetic properties can further delay climaxing by desensitising these areas.

Then there's **ecstasy** ▶

(MDMA) which is a psychedelic amphetamine in tablet form. Its effects can last several hours. 'E' enhances perceptions and sensations with an intensified pleasure in physical contact that leads to a greater desire for sex (though sometimes making it harder to come).

Possibly the most widely-used illicit drug, **cannabis** (whether eaten or smoked) heightens sensual and sexual awareness, although individual response is subjective, depending on mood, environment and expectations. Cannabis does appear to reduce inhibition, enhance impulses and feelings of intimacy, plus generally make sex more pleasurable and at least seem to last longer. Despite its prohibited status, medical evidence suggests that moderate occasional use produces practically no ill effects.

Amyl nitrite is now used primarily as a recreational drug. When inhaled, 'poppers' dilate the blood vessels and speed up the heart rate, so when taken during lovemaking, or just prior to orgasm, they can generate a dizzy sense of uninhibited elation.

The fact that they also relax the sphincter muscles goes some way to explaining their exalted status among the gay community.

Viagra rapidly became the fastest-selling drug in pharmaceutical history because, quite simply, it has helped produce impressive erections for millions of men, while some women have claimed it has helped to induce their first orgasms in years. Only time will tell whether or not Viagra really qualifies as the ultimate aphrodisiac.

folklore & more

The root of the **mandrake** was said to have powerful aphrodisiac properties if pulled from the ground at midnight. It was revered by the ancient Greeks as an ingredient in love potions and worn as a fertility amulet in medieval times, though it is little used today. Mandrake root has been found to contain atropine and scopolamine (both sedatives) and mandragorine (a hallucinogen) which could help to induce sexual fantasies.

It does seem extraordinary

that, in an attempt to attract the opposite sex, we can be persuaded by the perfume manufacturers to mask our natural body odours with the most bizarre combinations of animal secretions – even pig urine! A commonly used ingredient is **musk**, which is extracted from the sex glands of the musk deer.

For centuries it has been incorporated into medicine and potions to soothe the nerves and increase carnal desire. Recent research has shown that musk most closely resembles the smell of humans. Which begs the question, why bother to mask human odour with something akin to human odour?

Maybe we should just let those **pheromones** speak for themselves. There is, however, little scientific evidence to confirm the role of the pheromone (a unique chemical compound produced by all humans) in human sexual attraction. This hasn't stopped companies from cashing in by marketing isolated pheromones in sprays which they claim are irresistible to the opposite sex.

Scarcity has contributed to the mystique of powdered **rhino horn**: the Chinese were convinced that potions made from the horn of the rhinoceros would endow them with perpetual hard-ons. They also set great store by bear's gall bladder, tiger's penis and the like. Unfortunately, such ignorant Eastern superstition has lead to so many of these wonderful creatures being driven to the edge of extinction.

Finally, some aphrodisiacs should come with 'handle with extreme caution' warnings. The most notorious, **Spanish Fly** is a powder made from the dried bodies of the blister beetle (cantharis). When swallowed, it can generate great erections, but this is merely a reflex action to the irritation of the urethra and the discomfort doesn't simply subside after sex. Taken in even the most minute quantities, it can lead to dire consequences.

Though many products bear the name Spanish Fly, they aren't necessarily the genuine article – which is just as well.

PRUDES CORNER

While the USA may be a relatively progressive country, it has more laws regulating sexual behaviour than all the countries in the EU put together. Most European countries severed the ties between Church and State long ago, but US legislators feared that revisions in the old sex statutes would leave them open to accusations of immorality.

Hence the manufacture and sale of condoms was illegal in the USA until the end of 1930.

Alabama, Arizona, Florida, Georgia, Idaho, Louisiana, Minnesota, Mississippi, North & South Carolina, Oklahoma, Utah and Virginia: heterosexual anal sex, fellatio and cunnilingus were outlawed in all the above states as recently as 1990. Notice that the names of these states all end in a vowel?

Adultery laws still exist in around thirty American states.

In Nevada, it's illegal to have extramarital sex without a condom. Yet Nevada is the only state that sanctions prostitution; no surprise it boasts forty brothels, including the legendary Chicken Ranch.

The only lawful sexual position in Washington DC is face-to-face.

If it's not done in the missionary position, it ain't legit.

Strictly speaking, the only sex act that is legally sanctioned throughout the USA is heterosexual intercourse between married adults. In private.

Bad Vibes

In Texas, dildos can only be bought and sold only as 'novelties'. Stores there even make you sign a release form confirming that you will not be using the said novelty for sexual purposes, nor will you be explaining how to do so to others. Legislators in Alabama recently prohibited any device 'designed or marketed primarily for the stimulation of human genital organs'. In future, battery-driven Big Boy dildos will no doubt be promoted as gum massagers.

Every October, Berlin hosts a massive sexpo: The International Trade Fair for Internet, Multimedia and Adult Entertainment – better known simply as VENUS. It all began almost a decade ago as a small trade show but has since expanded to welcome the general public.

These days the seven huge halls of the Exhibition Grounds house 300 exhibitors from over 20 countries and attract 5,000 international traders plus over 20,000 consumers. Raunchy stage acts and adult industry stars abound and the annual Venus Awards Gala hands out gongs for all manner of XXX performances and dooberries, as well as electing a Miss Venus.

Having conquered Europe, Venus now has its sights set on China – the world's largest untapped adult market – with the nation's first sex fair in Shanghai in 2005.

London has its own four-day adult event, EROTICA, which has been running for ten years every November at Olympia.
Live stage shows, an erotic art gallery and over 100 stands – offering everything from sexy clothing and accessories to hardcore – entice tens of thousands of visitors to the UK's major adult shopping extravaganza.

THE JOY OF SEX **TOYS**

Once primly known as 'marital aids', sex toys have well and truly come out of the closet with an estimated £1billion spent world-wide last year on everything from designer dildos to nipple clamps and blow-up dolls. But did you know that...

The oldest known dildo is said to be 106,000 years old and was discovered in Iceland. Made of whalebone, it's inscribed with an ancient menstrual calendar. Fascinating Inuit?

70% of the world's sex toys are made in China and Hong Kong.

Battery powered may be more convenient, but mains-powered vibes are the most durable on the market, with some such as the Hitachi Magic Wand still giving good service twenty years down the line.

An estimated 20% of women use a vibrator while masturbating, and most women climax in under three minutes when they use one.

Though sex toys come in all shapes and sizes, there can be few more outrageous than a sacrilegious new range modelled upon biblical figures. The Virgin Mary dildo promises to

make a believer of you, whilst Moses can to lead you to the promised land. And whilst you may not have Christ in your heart, the Baby Jesus butt plug is nothing less than a divine intervention.

30% of strap-on sales are to heterosexual couples; a fact which gives lie to the notion that strap-ons are just for girl-on-girl fun.

You can buy artificial latex vaginas which are actually moulded from the most intimate bits of contemporary porn stars. So, if you're into sex toys which look like the type of thing Jack the Ripper might have favoured, you can take your pick from Tera Patrick's Futurotic Pussy & Ass and Sunset Thomas' Vibrating Realistic Vagina, amongst many others.

Cumbersome steam-powered vibrators first appeared in the USA in 1869 for the treatment of 'female disorders', but the first

'modern-style' battery-operated vibrator was designed by the British physician Joseph Granville in 1880 and mass produced by the Weiss company.

KY Jelly came onto the market as a lube in 1928, originally developed as an aid to physicians performing gynaecological examinations.

When it comes to sex dolls, westerners tend to opt for life-size 'realistic' figures, whilst orientals often prefer petite inflatables with cartoony faces. Maybe Hello Kitty ain't as innocent as she looks!

Penis pumps have been falsely marketed in the past as 'developers' which promise to increase penis size. In reality, what they do is to temporarily maximise your existing endowment. They operate by creating suction which draws blood into the penis, to give you a bigger and harder erection than normal.

The so-called Orgasmatron promises women almost guaranteed orgasms at the flick of a switch. Discovered by Dr Stuart Meloy who was originally researching a cure for back pain, the device is an electrode which is surgically implanted into the spinal column, which then allows you to 'turn yourself on' by remote control.

These days vibrators and dildos come in a variety of materials.
Jelly (polyvinyl chloride) is extremely flexible and bends to your body curves. *Plastic* is the least likely to absorb body fluids or react with your skin, but many people find it hard and inflexible. *Silicone* is popular but shouldn't be used with silicone-based lubes. *Acrylic* is used to create seamless, hard sex toys which are quick and easy to clean. *Glass* dildos are super-slick when they're lubed up. Glass also warms to your body but be wary, even a small nick in such a dildo can be hazardous. Incredibly realistic and lifelike vibrators and dildos are now made from specially developed, hi-tech trademarked materials such as *Technoskin* and *UR3*, which feel as similar to skin as you can get.

DIFFERENT STROKES

A **paraphilia** has been defined as 'a condition in men and women of being compulsively responsive to, or dependent upon, an unusual or socially unacceptable sexual stimulus'. Here are just a few...

acrotomophilia a sexual attraction to amputees

agalmatophilia a fetish for statues and mannequins (preferably nude)

agrexophilia arousal from the knowledge that others may see or hear their lovemaking

algophilia sexual arousal gained by pain sensations (such as biting), though not necessarily into SM

coprophilia refers to one who is turned on by faeces

doraphilia being stimulated by skin, leather and fur

dysmorphophilia arousal by deformities in partners such as scars or club feet, or by dwarves, hunchbacks, etc.

emetophilia a sexual fetish for throwing up and being vomited on (known by devotees as Roman showers)

formicophilia when having insects crawl over your genitals is a turn-on

gerontophilia an attraction for people who are significantly older, even elderly

hierophilia being stimulated by sacred objects (such as masturbating with a cross)

klismaphilia when enemas are a turn-on

lactaphilia arousal caused by lactating breasts

maieusiophilia a sexual attraction to pregnant women

podophilia a foot fetish

scopophilia a form of voyeurism, or being aroused by watching others engage in sexual/fetishistic activities

sitophilia refers to those who use food for sexual pleasure (whether cucumbers and corn-on-the-cob, or cream and honey)

somnophilia arousal from fondling or having sex with a partner who is asleep (assuming it is still consensual)

trichophilia a fetish for body hair (pubic, underarm or chest)

xenophilia a passion for sex only with strangers – effectively one-night stands

zoophilia sexual arousal from having sex with animals

SEX'N'SHOPPING

A sexual **phobia** (fear or aversion) may be caused by guilt, temporary stress, problems with intimacy or a negative experience. It can range from mild anxiety to a panic attack. Below are some examples:

automysophobia fear of getting dirty
coitophobia fear of sexual intercourse
dishabiliophobia fear of undressing in front of others
erotophobia fear of sexual intimacy
eurotophobia fear of female genitals
gymnophobia fear of nudity
medorthophobia fear of the erect penis
naphephobia fear of touch
paraphobia fear of sexual perversions

■ While it is now perfectly legal to buy hardcore R18 videos and DVDs, they are available only from licensed sex shops. Problem is, there are less than 300 such shops nationwide. That's just one shop per 200,000 people.

■ Sex shop licenses are granted by local authorities, who may choose to deny all applications in their area, so there is none in Northern Ireland. Yet there are around twenty in London's West End alone, even though the cost of a licence can run to £30,000 per year. A nice little earner for Westminster council!

■ Britain's largest adult store is Hustler Hollywood in Birmingham, at a sprawling 6,000 square feet.

■ Ann Summers, the 'pleasure retailer', has over 120 shops across the UK, but being non-licensed, they major in lingerie, fantasy wear, potions, lotions and toys.

She was England's biggest sex star of the 1970s, appearing in countless photo spreads, hardcore shorts and sex comedies. She was the girl next door, who just happened to like a lot of sex...

Mary Millington's life story is liberally sprinkled with sex parties, mounds of drugs, scandal, porn barons, celebrity nookie, plus lusty trysts for cash and gifts: she was one busy woman! A former Miss Dorking, Mary made her modelling debut in 1970, which led to what were known at the time as 'Swedish' movies. Two years before *Deep Throat*, Mary was making hardcore that, to paraphrase porn baron David Sullivan, 'made Linda Lovelace look like Noddy!'

It was Sullivan who turned her into a household name. Her bit parts in low-budget British sexploitation films such as *Eskimo Nell*, and *I'm Not Feeling Myself Tonight*, together with her reputation as a hardcore player and glamour girl extraordinaire, gave him one of his greatest money-making ideas. Exploiting her top-shelf notoriety to the max, he billed her as the star in his own saucy feature film *Come Play With Me*, though her appearances in the movie were fleeting. Released in 1977, it ran continuously at Soho's Classic Moulin cinema for four years and established her as a star.

Escort work and sex parties were part of her undeclared earnings and she bonked the rich and famous, from premier-league footballers to celebrities. By 1976 she was multi-tasking further, flouting the law selling hardcore from her own sex shop.

Fame came with a price: Mary drew the attention of the police and the taxman, leading to problems with depression and drugs.

Eventually, panicked by a tax demand for a million pounds and feeling harassed by the Obscene Publications Squad, she took an overdose in 1979 at the age of just 34, leaving a suicide note pleading for the laws on porn to be amended.

MARY QUEEN OF HOTS

YOU WANT ME TO DO **WHAT?**

At a casting session, it's best to have a grasp of porno parlance, so you know just what you might be in for...

Back Spackle Shooting cum over the back or buttocks.

Bukkake A porn sub-genre which involves groups of men ejaculating on the face of, or in the mouth of, a female performer.

Cream Pie When cum can be seen dripping from the vagina or anus.

DA Is double anal or two cocks up the bum at once. Ouch!

DP Double penetration or entered front and back at the same time.

Facial The standard routine of ejaculating onto the face of the female star.

Fluffer A woman who helps get the males hard before they go on camera, by giving them BJs.

IP Internal 'pop shot' or ejaculation.

Money Shot The male ejaculation captured on film. So called, because male performers are apparently paid depending on their ability to deliver said shot.

Reverse Cowgirl Sex position with the woman on top, facing away from the man, towards the camera. A porno staple which maximises the view of penetration.

Reverse Gangbang No, not a group of women having their way with a man, unfortunately, but rather where one man takes on several women at the same time or in quick succession.

Snowballing Also known as 'cum swapping', where ejaculate is passed from one mouth to another, or simply kissing someone after they have received a gobful of man juice.

Spit-Roast When a woman is penetrated from behind while she's performing oral on a guy in front, so looking like she is impaled on two cocks.

Suitcase Pimp Disparaging term which refers to a starlet's unemployed boyfriend or husband, who carries her suitcase onto a film set. SPs are often to be seen talking into a mobile phone trying to look important, and generally acting as an 'agent'.

Teabagging This is where the testicles are lowered onto a performer's face or into the mouth. It also refers to sucking on a man's balls. It's the taste, you know!

COSMIC SEX

So what's Tantric Sex all about, then? Is it some hippy fad made famous by Sting? Or is it really the pathway to erotic nirvana?

Tantric sex promises multiple orgasms for men and women. Male ejaculation is prohibited as it wastes sexual energy. Women are encouraged to ejaculate as much as possible. The average sex act takes 10 minutes. Tantric sex can take hours.

Tantric sex is a complex marriage of yoga, meditation, ritual and sex. It was originally practised by Tibetian, Chinese and Indian Buddists who saw it as a sacred act. It united their spirit with the flesh and enabled them to achieve enlightenment. A vagina is called a *yoni* (sacred space) and a penis is a *lingham* (wand of light). So rather than asking your partner, 'Fuck me with your monster,' it is more Tantric to suggest 'Enter my sacred space with your wand of light'. Hmmm...

The basic belief is that energy flows through the body, connecting the *chakras* (energy centres) which include the base of the spine, the crown of the head, the forehead, the throat, the stomach and the genitals. The aim is to channel energy through these *chakras* which promotes oneness and ecstasy. And this can be achieved by reaching a high level of sexual arousal.

And there are no ordinary sex positions either.
Where Western sex has the old missionary, doggy and girl-on-top combos, tantric sex really goes to town:
They have 'The Fitting of the Sock', 'Pounding on the Spot', 'Frog Fashion', 'Fixing of a Nail' and 'The Tail of the Ostrich'.

LIBIDO **LOCO**

The average man desires sex twice as much as the average woman according to a recent study, which has concluded that on average, the male body clock is set to a five-day cycle when it comes to wanting sex, while women are on a ten-day cycle.

In plain speak, that means that men crave sex five days after they last had it, whereas women could quite happily go without it for a further five days. This sexual imbalance can then become exacerbated even further if a woman responds to her man's needs and agrees to have sex halfway through her natural cycle. Effectively, this puts her libidinal clock back to zero and the process begins again. As a consequence, her experience of sex will be unsatisfactory and as she never reaches her optimum tenth day, she can begin to feel that she has lost her libido completely. Crikey!

But on the bright side, whilst women generally anticipate a drop in sexual desire following the menopause, many report that the opposite is true, as unencumbered by concerns about pregnancy and contraception, their libido hits a new high. Hurrah!

HOT LICKS & TONGUE TRICKS

Below are a few oral techniques which will go down very well with the lucky lady on the receiving end.

- ⇩ Use your tongue in different ways: it can be soft, light and pointed, or it can have a focused, firm tip. Be sure not to inadvertently poke her clitoris with too much pressure.
- ⇩ Cover her vulva with your entire mouth.
- ⇩ Nibble the outer and inner lips, or the clitoral hood.
- ⇩ Learn the 'ice cream lick'. Make your tongue flat and wide, and lick her vulva like a melting ice cream cone. These licks can feel very good when they're firm.
- ⇩ Explore with your tongue by tracing out each letter of the alphabet.
- ⇩ She may enjoy having her clitoris sucked, but keep in mind that it's not for everyone. If she's really hot, combine the suction with your tongue gently pushing her clit in and out, side to side, up and down, or circling it.
- ⇩ Try gently taking her clit in your teeth and holding it, lightly flicking with your tongue.
- ⇩ Penetrate her vagina with your stiff tongue; this is known as tongue fucking. Not all women go crazy for it – if she's really aroused it may not provide a firm enough stimulation — but some will enjoy it in the beginning stages of cunnilingus.
- ⇩ When your mouth makes full contact, try moaning appreciatively – your mouth and tongue will vibrate her vulva, a delicious sensation in itself.

For more, see *The Ultimate Guide to Cunnilingus* by Violet Blue (Cleis) £7.99

THE BIGGEST DICK IN THE WORLD

The biggest dick in the world belongs to
Cerne Abbas man. Carved out of a limestone
hillside in Dorset, he sports a mammoth
erection, 26 feet long.

Also known as the 'Rude Man', his origins
are shrouded in mystery, though many
historians believe that the figure is a Roman
representation of Hercules dating back
around 2,000 years.

The story goes that a woman who spends a
night on the hill with her lover – within the
outline of the rampant phallus – dramatically
increases her chances of conceiving.
Consequently, the inhabitants of this small
Dorset town ensure the grass never grows
too long to obscure their Jolly Green Giant's
mighty weapon.

**Since the figure stands at 180 feet tall, a
quick calculation reveals that, if reduced
to human proportions, his cock measures a
good 10 inches.**

LOVE FOR SALE

Prostitution may be the world's oldest profession, but the rules, regulations and opinions regarding it are still far from straightforward.

■ Things started out promisingly: in ancient Babylon, prostitutes were considered sacred and plied their trade in religious temples where they acted as 'wives of God'. Their earnings accounted for a substantial part of the income of the temples. And in India, the similar tradition of the *devadasi*, or temple whore, continued right up until the late 19th century.

> Construction has begun on a massive brothel in Berlin, scheduled to open in 2006, in time to welcome thousands of football fans attending the World Cup in Germany. It's claimed the Artemis mega-brothel will have a sauna, lap-dancing bar and 100 rooms. Admission will be 100 euros, plus 50 euros for half an hour with your lady of choice.

■ Of course those horny ancient Greeks had their own take on this: the first state-licensed brothels were set up by Athenian lawmaker Solon in 594BC who cannily placed a tax on what he regarded as an essential service. Surprisingly, this was initially a slow starter, but eventually caught on as soliciting women began to take off more clothes!

■ In 100BC, Roman poet and philosopher Lucretius passed on a rather doubtful form of birth control learned by observing prostitutes (presumably at rather close quarters). He noted the bump'n'grind employed by these women of the night did more than produce pleasure: it also averted semen from its course thus avoiding unwanted pregnancy. However, he recommended that such depraved behaviour stayed outside the marital bed: 'This our wives surely have no need of!'

■ As well as teaching 'birth control', prostitutes have been used at times for other forms of social control: in the fifteenth century, the Doge of Venice (chief magistrate), decreed

> Back in Victorian times, chaps who made themselves available to women were known as Fancy men. These old-school gigolos were often law or medical students who were kept by older, well-heeled women. Under English law a man cannot be a prostitute, 'common' or otherwise, as the term is only legally recognised in relation to women, although rent boys can be prosecuted for soliciting.

that Venetian prostitutes must bare their breasts whilst plying for trade, in order to divert the city's young men from homosexuality. There's no record as to whether or not this worked but all of the straight guys must have walked around in heaven in the meantime!

■ The notion of sex as sinful finally reared its ugly head. In 1545, Henry VIII took a break from beheading his wives to decree that England's brothels (officially sanctioned by the state since 1161) must now close down. The growing fear of syphilis made this easy for the king to institute without too much protest.

In 1566 Pope Pius V expelled prostitutes from the papal states, and by 1588 Henry III decreed that all harlots must leave Paris within 24 hours or face a public flogging.

■ The red-light district has long been a recognisable feature of most cities. Storyville in New Orleans was the home of one of the world's biggest red-light districts, which in 1900 stretched over 38 blocks. But in 1857, city fathers decided that something had to be done about rife prostitution. So they legalised it. Sadly this also involved taxing the workers.

One brothel owner was so fed up with this that she sued the city's government, and the court found in her favour, leading to a week-long celebration by the hookers. Adds a whole new dimension to 'girl power'.

■ Today, laws surrounding prostitution are as confusing as ever.

It is not illegal in Germany, Netherlands, Austria, Japan, Brazil, Peru, Turkey and the state of Nevada, USA. France had state-licensed brothels since the time of Napoleon right up until 1946, when they had a change of heart; and Italy closed the doors on their bordellos in 1958.

QUICKIES...

If you've ever wondered what all those abbreviations stand for in the more risqué personals columns and in contact ads, now you can crack the swingers' code. However, we should remind you that a few, such as ALA, NS and SAE, are really quite tame!

AC/DC
bisexual
ALA
all letters answered
A
anal sex
B&D
bondage & discipline
BDSM
bondage & discipline, dominance & submission, and sadomasochism
bi
bisexual
CP
corporal punishment
CTOA
can travel or accommodate
D&S
dominance & submission
DIY
masturbation
dom
dominant
GB
gangbang
GSOH
good standard of health
GSOL
good standard of living

LTR
longterm relationship
M/F
male/ female
NS
non-smokers
O
oral sex
S
spanking
SAE
stamped addressed envelope
S&M, S/M, SM
sadomasochism
sub
submissive
TS
transsexual
TV
cross-dresser
tied
married
UD
nude (undraped)
vas
vasectomised
WLTM
would like to meet
WS
watersports
WE
well-endowed

THE PAGES OF SIN

A cent a word or a dollar a page? No matter – in the 1940s, both **Henry Miller** (1891–1980) and **Anaïs Nin** (1903–1977) wrote erotica for 'patrons', which is a nice way of saying that, when they were hard up, they penned wanking material for rich clients. Nin was in the USA where Miller put her in touch with a 'private collector'. He later turned out to be an underground publisher who simply made copies of her erotic short stories and sold them on. Although the permanently broke Miller's reputation was established with *Tropic of Cancer*, Nin's was yet to come.

Eventually it was her diaries that gained her literary recognition but, ironically, it was her pay-per-page porn that made her as famous as Miller when *Delta of Venus* was published shortly after her death. It was only because she wanted both her surviving husband and her lover to benefit that she finally sold these erotic short stories, little knowing they would be on the *New York Times* best-seller list for 36 weeks or be translated into 26 different languages.

Nin's tortuous *ménage à trois* with Miller and his wife was later portrayed in the movie *Henry and June*.

In 1954, *Story of O* appeared under the pseudonym of Pauline Réage, published simultaneously by the Olympia Press in English and by Jean-Jacques Pauvert in French. The author was Dominique Aury (1907–1998), a highly respectable 47- year-old intellectual who worked for top Paris publishers, Gallimard. She wrote her now-classic SM novel as a challenge for her lover, Jean Paulhan.

At first banned in France, it subsequently gained national recognition and spawned a hilarious movie version by *Emmanuelle* director, Just Jaecklin, in which one of the central characters is repeatedly referred to as 'Sir Stiffun'.

> The anus is tightly packed with nerve cells, similar to those found in the clitoris or penis. The anus is approximately four degrees warmer than the vagina and has over eight working muscles.

Anal sex: the Holy Grail of the sexual world. It seems that everyone – gay or straight, male or female – is either talking about or taking part in a bit of bum sex. Love it or hate it, anal sex must have something going for it as our ancestors have been indulging for centuries.

Together with the fact that anal sex can be very enjoyable for both partners, it probably originated from its practice as a form of birth control.

Those cavemen invented some wondrous things. Fire: check. The wheel: check. Anal sex: check.

For the Ancient Greeks, sexual love between men was considered perfectly normal and anal sex was positively encouraged. In fact, they were so keen on it, the term 'Greek love' was used to refer to the practice, and in modern times, 'Greek' is still sometimes used as slang for anal sex.

However in 342AD, the Emperors Constantius and Constans went and spoiled everyone's fun by prohibiting both oral and anal sex.

UP YER BUM!

In several cultures and countries (such as the Mediterranean area and Latin America), heterosexual anal sex is widely accepted because of the lower risk of unwanted pregnancy. It is also sometimes seen as a way of preserving virginity until marriage. So, that ought to please your husband: your vagina has never known a man's touch, yet half of Brazil has been up your bottom.

Some medieval woodcuts show people kissing the anus of a goat-like figure representing the Devil. He's obviously a big fan of rimming. In other cultures, notably Japan, records (including detailed woodblock prints) show men merrily rogering each other up the bottom. In 18th century England, another term for anal sex was 'to navigate the windward passage'. Charming.

So how many people have actually had anal sex? It seems that some might be a little ashamed of how filthy they are as there are several discrepancies in the results of different researchers. For example, Edward O Laumann's *The Social Organization of Sexuality: Sexual Practices in the United States* found that about 20% of heterosexuals have engaged in anal sex, but sex researcher Alfred Kinsey found that number to be closer to 40%. More recently, a researcher from the University of British Columbia puts the number of heterosexuals who regularly practice anal sex at between 30% and 50%. That's more like it.

VICTORIAN VICE

Bawdy joke circulating when Queen Victoria married Albert in 1840:
1st Gent: 'So Albert goes with the Queen to Windsor after the ceremony?'
2nd Gent: 'Oh, further than that. He'll go in at Bushey, pass Virginia Water, on through Maidenhead and leave Staines behind.'

Still considered to be the high tide of British sexual hypocrisy and responsible for many of our sexual hang-ups of today, the Victorian age (1837-1901) has been demonised as a strait-laced and repressive era. But the reality was more complex than that.

As levels of population and education increased, there was a huge demand for inexpensive pornographic literature and pictures; new, cheaper printing processes, such as lithography and photography, were able to satisfy this need.

An army of prostitutes of all ages existed (as many as 80,000 in London alone), ready to cater for every sexual whim. It was a time of extremes: highly enjoyable for the rich sexual predator, but indescribably nasty for the single, destitute female.

These two social problems, **pornography** and **prostitution**, were dealt with by the

VICTORIAN VICE

Victorians in curiously eccentric ways. The elderly Lord Chief Justice, Lord Campbell, staggered to his feet during a Lord's debate on poisons, and told his audience that there were 'far greater dangers to society than those caused by the misuse of poisons: I have learned with horror and alarm that a sale of poison more deadly than prussic acid, strychnine or arsenic – the sale of obscene publications and indecent books – is openly going on...'

Subsequently, the Obscene Publications Act of 1857 was passed and the pornography and erotica trades that had flourished openly in the print shops of London's Holywell Street were driven underground. Those found guilty by this new law were given draconian sentences. Only academics and aristocrats seemed able pursue their erotic interests with some degree of immunity.

In 1885 William Stead, the editor of the *Pall Mall Gazette*, purchased 13-year-old chimney sweep's daughter, Eliza Armstrong, for five pounds, showing how easy it was to procure a virgin for prostitution. Stead wrote up his investigations and the outcry this caused was enormous. Even though Stead was supported by the moral majority, he was still charged with unlawfully kidnapping a minor. He was found guilty on a technicality and was imprisoned for three months. But as a result of the publicity generated, Parliament raised the age of consent from 13 to 16 and strengthened existing legislation against prostitution.

THE PLEASURE ZONE

Given the right touch, lick or nibble, a woman's whole body is one big erogenous zone and different women prefer their body to be caressed in different ways and places, though not necessarily all at once. For those of you who prefer a more scientific approach, here's her top hot spots, in descending order:

Clitoris Has as many nerve endings as the glans of the penis. However, they are packed together much more tightly, meaning the clitoris is more sensitive. Unlike the penis, the clit has only one function – pleasure. There is a God!

G-Spot A pea-sized mass of nerve tissue located two to three inches inside the vagina on the front wall. Compared to the male prostate gland, stimulation can cause female ejaculation.

Labia While the outer lips (labia majora) of the vulva are the least excitable parts of female genitals, the inner lips (labia minora) are far more sensitive.

Vagina About 4 inches deep but very stretchy. The front wall has more nerve endings than the back wall.

Anus Packed with nerve endings and extremely responsive to sexual stimulation.

Buttocks If you've ever wondered why many women enjoy a gentle (or in some cases not so gentle) spanking, it's due to the 'butterfly' structure of the clitoris. The clitoris splits into two wings which extend back around the walls of the vagina and these are stimulated by pressure to the buttocks and back of thighs. Bend over, please.

Breasts and Nipples During arousal, breasts swell and nipples become erect as blood flow to the area increases. So, the next time she complains her breasts are too small, you'll be able to lend a helping hand, or mouth, or tongue…

Lips and Mouth Lips are 100 times more sensitive than the fingertips and the average person spends two weeks of their life kissing. Although a passionate kiss can also shorten your life by up to a minute, due to increased hormone levels in the blood.

Fingers and Toes As our main touching device, fingers are particularly sensitive and a relatively large area of the brain is reserved for receiving information from them; the same goes for feet and toes.

SHAVING RYAN'S PRIVATES

For anyone under the impression that you don't need a creative bone in your body to produce a porn movie, think again. Somewhere out there is a crack team of some of Hollywood's finest brains, otherwise known as the Porn Movie Namers. Such wit, such originality, such style. PMNs – we salute you!

A Tale of Two Titties
An Officer and a Genitalman
An Orifice and a Gentleman
The Bare Bitch Project
Beverley Hills Copulator
Buttman & Throbbin'
Das Booty
Dildo Baggins: Lord of the Wangs
Dirty Toy Story
Forrest Hump
Good Willy Humping
Harry's Hotter with the Philosopher's Bone
How The West Was Hung
Glad He Ate Her
Jurassic Pork
Lawrence of a Labia
Lap Dances with Wolves
Malcolm XXX
Night of the Giving Head
On Golden Blonde
Phallus in Wonderland
Pornocchio
Shaving Ryan's Privates
Shavers of the Lost Arse
The Sexorcist
The Sperminator
Whore of the Worlds
Willy Wanker & the Fudge Packing Factory

CARNAL CURIO COLLECTIONS

Nowadays you can find a sex museum of one kind or another in most major cities, from Berlin to New York. Even London is getting in on the act, with a sex museum proposed for the Trocadero centre near Piccadilly Circus in 2006. However, here are two museums unlike any other.

Deep in the heart of Prague's Old City, you can find evidence – if you ever doubted it – that sex and science have walked hand in hand down the centuries. The Museum of Sex Machines has 200 exhibits on three floors, celebrating the fact that sex aids long predate the present battery-driven era. According to curator Lucie

Poricka (pictured right with vintage steam-driven dildo), the museum drew 300,000 visitors last year in search of amusement, titillation and some eye-opening education. Interestingly, the items on display reveal ingenuity applied both to assisting erotic arousal and preventing it. For every great mind working on a hand-cranked vibrator or hot water-filled dildo, there was an uptight doppleganger beavering away on an electrical anti-masturbation machine or a saw-toothed chastity belt.

The Icelandic Phallological Museum in Husavik boasts an array of over one hundred and fifty specimens of penises and penile parts belonging to almost every land and sea mammal in Iceland, together with a collection of phallic art. This is probably the only museum in the world to have such a comprehensive collection of such, er, national treasures. Founder and director Sigurdur Hjartarson's claims all this enables serious academic study of the phallus, in a land where male genitalia are usually severely shrunken by the cold.

If it weren't for pickpockets, I'd have
no sex life at all.
Rodney Dangerfield

I have so little sex appeal that my
gynaecologist calls me sir.
Joan Rivers

You know, of course, that the Tasmanians, who never
committed adultery, are now extinct.
W Somerset Maugham

In general, I think it's true that women fuck
to love, and men love to fuck
Carrie Fisher

I believe that sex is a beautiful thing between two
people. Between five, it's fantastic...
Woody Allen

Chastity is the most unnatural of all
the sexual perversions.
Remy de Gourmont

I regret to say that we of the FBI are powerless to act
in cases of oral-genital intimacy,
unless it has in some way
obstructed interstate commerce.
J Edgar Hoover

The good thing about masturbation is that
you don't have to dress up for it.
Truman Capote

►

There are a number of mechanical devices which increase sexual arousal, particularly in women. Chief among these is the Mercedes-Benz 380SL convertible.
PJ O'Rourke

Life can little more supply,
Than just a few good fucks, and then we die.
Thomas Potter, attrib, John Wilkes MP

If God intended us not to masturbate, He would have made our arms shorter.
George Carlin

I'm glad I'm not bisexual. I don't think I could handle being rejected by men as well as women.
Bernard Manning

It is now quite lawful for a Catholic woman to avoid pregnancy by a resort to mathematics, though she is still forbidden to resort to physics and chemistry.
HL Mencken

I know nothing about sex, because I was always married.
Zsa Zsa Gabor

Really, Madam! You must be more careful! What if someone else had found you like this?
Duc de Richelieu, on finding his wife with her lover

TALKING SEX

Are you going to come quietly or do I have to use earplugs?
The Goon Show

Marriage is the tomb of love.
Giovanni Jacopo Casanova

I've had my cock sucked by the biggest names in Hollywood.
James Dean

Men aren't attracted to me by my mind. They're attracted
to me by what I don't mind.
Gypsy Rose Lee

Dildoes and dogs with women do prevail,
I caught one frigging with a cur's bobtail:
My Lord, said she, I do it with remorse,
For once I had a passion for a horse.
The Earl of Rochester

You know the worst thing about oral sex? The view.
Maureen Lipman

I'm a practising heterosexual... but bisexuality immediately
doubles your chances for a date on a Saturday night.
Woody Allen

Yes, I admit that I am a libertine and in that area I have imagined
everything that can be imagined. But I have certainly not
acted out everything that I imagined, nor do I intend to. I am a
libertine, not a criminal or a murderer.
Marquis de Sade

PENILE DEMENTIA

■ **Lorena Bobbitt grew tired of the poor sexual performance and abusive behaviour of her husband, John Wayne Bobbitt, and on 23 June 1993, she cut off his knob with a butcher's knife. She ditched his dick in an empty lot. Police soon found the severed organ, and it was successfully reattached.**

When questioned by police as to why she chopped off his chopper, Lorena responded, 'He always has an orgasm and never waits for me. It's unfair.' She was subsequently acquitted on grounds of temporary insanity.

John went on (in this order) to make pornographic videos; to minister to a church; and to drive a truck. Most recently, he went to court to reclaim the knife from police storage, in the hope of selling it on eBay.

■ Grigori Rasputin, healer and mystic, delighted the ladies of the Imperial Court in St Petersburg with his 13-inch penis. Widely unpopular among people outside of the Romanov's inner circle, he was castrated and murdered in 1916.

The penis was lost, then recovered by his maid in his apartment. The organ then travelled with his daughter Marie throughout South America. After her death in California in 1997, it was sold to Michael Augustine. In 1994, it was auctioned with the remainder of Marie's possessions for £350.

Rasputin's preserved cock is now back in St Petersburg, on display at the Museum of Erotica.

SILENT PARTNERS

■ Ever since Pymalion carved Galatea out of ivory, man has craved uncomplicated female companionship. Some Victorian sea captains equipped their crews with a rubber sex doll or *dame de voyage* for the same reason (and no doubt this cut down on shipboard buggery); the only problems were those of sexually-transmitted diseases and squabbles over what her favourite cocktail was.

■ Hitler is said to have ordered the development of an inflatable sex doll (one in every stormtrooper's rucksack in the name of preserving Aryan 'purity'), however no corroborative records exist.

■ Once in mass-production, the sex doll became an essential accessory to all stag parties, occasionally ending up perched atop a lofty civic edifice.

It boggles the mind that people actually attempt to have sex with these anatomically bizarre inflations when the experience must surely come very close to trying to shag a vinyl beach ball.

■ It's true, latex dolls were better (and about five times more pricey) but the quantum leap in sex doll technology was made by a firm called RealDoll. Manufactured in California (where else?), these silicone sweeties, costing around four grand, really are the stripper's merkin when it comes to 'realistic love dolls'. The customer can even play God and create the girl of his dreams, choosing everything about the way she looks, right down to eye shadow.

■ Competition is hotting up, with Japan now producing *anime* cartoon-inspired life-sized dolls; and Germany, too, getting back into the act with a doll that increases its temperature and breathing rate during intercourse. Moaning probably comes extra, though.

THE **SEX** DOCTORS

What is sexology? Well, it's an 'ology' and that makes it a science, and it's about sex, so really it's the science of sex. Sexologists systematically study human sexuality and attempt to classify 'normal' sexuality as well as 'abnormal' sexuality. The difficult part is, what was once considered perverted and deranged enough to earn you a life sentence in a padded cell, would now scarcely raise an eyebrow.

Richard Freiherr von Krafft-Ebing (1840-1902)

He is commonly acknowledged as one of the earliest known sexologists. A German physician, in 1886 he published *Psychopathia Sexualis* in which he catalogued a huge number of sexual 'perversities'. Although homosexuality was a crime in Germany and the Austro-Hungarian Empire at the time, Krafft-Ebing reached the conclusion that homosexuality was a sexual inversion of the brain which occurred while the individual was still in the womb. Homosexuals were normal people, but with a different sexuality. This was extremely advanced and controversial thinking for those days when people wanted to believe that homosexuality was a disease or psychological problem. He is famous for coining the term 'sadism' after studying the sexual pleasure achieved by inflicting harm and pain on others.

He also got into trouble with the Catholic Church for daring to suggest that the desire for sanctity and martyrdom were synonymous with masochism, where people achieved sexual pleasure from receiving punishment. With all that kneeling and praying and penance, you can understand his point.

Sigmund Freud (1856-1939)

He is maybe considered the most influential psychological theorist of 20th-century. Freud's fundamental idea was that all humans are endowed with an unconscious in which potent sexual and aggressive drives, and defences against them, struggle for supremacy.

He also developed his theory of the Oedipus Complex where children develop a sexual attraction towards a parent of the same sex while competing with the parent of the opposite sex. Steady on there, Freud, isn't that just nasty?

Freud's theories are often treated with scepticism. Not only did he not really have any scientific data to back up his theories, he was also rumoured to be fond of the old Colombian marching powder, and some have even suggested that this psychoanalysis lark was an excuse to shag his prettier 'patients'. Nice work if you can get it.

Henry Havelock Ellis (1859-1939)

Ellis was a British doctor interested in sexual liberation. He challenged the view that masturbation was abnormal, and was the first to suggest many common sexual 'problems' of the day such as homosexuality and masturbation, were merely normal sexual deviations.

Sex lies at the root of life, and we can never learn to reverence life until we know how to understand sex.

It was rumoured Ellis was a virgin for much of his life and only achieved full sexual arousal in late middle age when his wife urinated on him.

Dr Alfred Charles Kinsey (1894-1956)

A professor of entomology and zoology, Kinsey (right) founded the Institute for Sex Research in 1947 at Indiana University, now commonly known as the Kinsey Institute. His parents were extremely conservative Christians and as a child Kinsey was forbidden to know anything about the subject he would one day become famous for.

He was interested in how wide the variation of sexual practices in humans were and proposed that people do not fall neatly into hetero- ▶

or homosexual categories. He also believed that delayed sexual experience was psychologically harmful.

The groundbreaking Kinsey Reports on male and female sexuality caused a wave of controversy, especially in the Christian Church who believed that they were a morally corrupting force. However they profoundly influenced social and cultural values in the United States, especially in the 1960s and were an important factor in the sexual revolution. In the 1960s the American Psychological Association removed homosexuality from its list of mental illnesses as a result of Kinsey's Reports.

Kinsey has since been described as a bisexual masochist and is reported to have indulged in group sex and filming private pornographic videos. Fair enough.

Wilheim Reich (1897-1957)

A pupil of Freud, he got into a spot of bother by daring to suggest that every individual should have a healthy and satisfying sex life. The very idea! This was 1950s America after all. But he couldn't keep his mouth shut and went on to suggest that lack of a really good shag and orgasm could inhibit the life force, or 'orgone' as he termed it. What's more, he had built an 'Orgone Box' to replenish those who felt they had dwindling supplies. One can only imagine what went on in that box. Sounds fun though. The spoilsports at the Food and Drug Administration didn't think so, and ordered Reich to destroy all these scary Orgone Box thingies that had the capacity to turn normal, respectable civilians into raging perverts.

When one of Reich's associates was caught smuggling an orgone box across state lines, Reich himself was sentenced to two years in jail and all his books, research and equipment was destroyed. He died in prison in 1957.

It is said that Reich's first sexual experience was watching the maid and coachman going at it, and that he was later 'educated' by his nurse.

STICKY ENDS

Here are some true tales of the untimely deaths of movie folk in Porno Babylon

Murder

Japanese bondage star, **Nozomi Momoi**, was stabbed to death in a bizarre murder-suicide pact in 2002.

The **Mitchell Brothers** made the classic porn movie, 1972's *Behind the Green Door*. But any brotherly love was long gone by 1991, when Jim Mitchell shot his brother Artie dead.

Porn actress **Taylor Summers** was stabbed to death in 2004 following a bondage photo shoot. Her body was discovered with multiple stab wounds and a ball gag in her mouth. The photographer was charged with murder and abuse of a corpse.

Billy London, gay star of *Bulge* and *Hard Choices*, was discovered dismembered in a garbage can on Santa Monica Boulevard in 1990.

Suicide

Porn actor and talent-spotter **Rex Cabo** committed suicide in 2005, by jumping off the eleventh floor of a building in Long Beach, California, landing on a police car. Cabo discovered porn star Savannah, who shot herself in 1994 after a car accident left her face disfigured.

Wendy O' Williams, lead singer of The Plasmatics, gave a memorable performance shooting eggs out of her pussy in the 1979 film *Candy Goes to Hollywood*. She shot herself in the head in 1998.

Cal Jammer, stud and ex-husband of porn queen Jill Kelly, died of self-inflicted gunshot wounds in '95.

Misadventure

In 2004, bisexual adult star, **Fabio Scorpion**, died of a heart attack in surgery, for calf implants!

Tom Farrell died in 1993 in a hit-and-run as he was urinating by the side of the road.

Aids

Gay star **Sparky O'Toole** officially died of Aids in 1999. Frankly, we think it was more likely that he died of shame, on account of his name!

Mystery

A question mark hangs over the demise of **Bambi Woods**, star of *Debbie Does Dallas*. Did she die of a drug overdose in 1986, did she disappear and take on a new identity?

HIGH-FLYING SEX INNOVATOR

German sex pioneer **Beate Uhse** lived the life of which movies are made. She opened the world's first sex shop in 1962, and is also credited with almost single-handedly liberating her homeland in the postwar years from its many Nazi-inspired sexual taboos.

A former Luftwaffe captain, she flew planes to the front during the war. And after brief imprisonment in England, Uhse returned to Germany to found Europe's largest adult empire, active in twelve countries, with an annual turnover of around £100m.

She started out in 1946, selling a family-planning brochure door-to-door to uninformed German women (Nazi doctrine had dictated that contraception was the greatest evil), and by 1999, her company Beate Uhse AG was floated on the Frankfurt stock exchange. Along the way, she fought numerous battles with the authorities, who in the early days tried to stop her selling condoms to unwed couples, alongside devices to improve potency.

Legal proceedings were instigated against her more than 2,000 times, though remarkably she only ever lost one case. In contrast to such reactionary hysteria, her own pragmatic attitude to matters carnal can be summed up in her words: 'Sex, like eating and drinking, is one of mankind's basic needs.' Amen to that! This remarkable woman lived to the age of 81 and shuffled off this mortal coil in 2001.

THE UPLIFTING STORY OF THE BRA

■ **Jean Harlow**, the original platinum blonde bomb-shell, was the first star to regularly appear in movies without a bra. And she kept ice cubes at hand on set to keep her nipples hard. **Marilyn Monroe** never wore panties on or off the film set. Yet she always wore a bra at night to bed, in the belief it might prevent sagging breasts.

■ One of the most celebrated bras was created in the 1940s for Hollywood star **Jane Russell**, to wear in *The Outlaw* to accentuate her cleavage. Designed by Howard Hughes, the film director and eccentric aviation tycoon, the 'cantilevered' (push-up) bra proved so uncomfortable that Russell never actually wore it in the film.

■ For her Blonde Ambition tour in 1990, **Madonna** sported her famed 'bullet' bra, created by couture designer, Jean Paul Gaultier. It later fetched over £14,000 at auction.

■ The most popular bra size is 36B, yet professional fitters claim that 75% of women wear the wrong size. Clearly their cups runneth over.

■ The all-time best-selling bra goes by the homely name of **Doreen**. With a functional cross-your-heart style, it was launched by Triumph back in 1967, yet still plays a major supporting role today.

Storm in a D-cup
In 1994, Gossard's Wonderbra advertising on billboards ('Hello, boys!') was a sensation, and boosted the career of model Eva Herzigova. But the advertising campaign was promptly condemned by the Royal Society for the Prevention of Accidents, who claimed they distracted male drivers, and led to car crashes... Hello, lampost!

WHO LIVES IN A PLACE LIKE THIS?

Titter ye not, for at some time, somebody, somewhere, thought it would be a fine idea to give their hometown a name like some of these. Imagine the sense of civic pride in announcing, 'Howdy, folks! I'm the new Mayor of Bumpass…'

United Kingdom

In Southern England you'll find: Shootup Hill, Pratts Bottom, Willey, Great Bulging and Thong.

In the Midlands there are two places called Bell End.

The North rejoices in such names as Slack Bottom, Cockup Hill, Great Cockup, Little Cockup, Dirtpot, Bushygap and Knob End.

The Scottish Isles have two Twatts, while Lord Berkeley's Knob is located in mainland Scotland.

And Northern Ireland has one solitary Muff.

Canada

While the rest of Canada is pretty staid, Newfoundland takes the prize with Dildo, South Dildo, Conception Harbour and Pecker's Point.

Australia

They nicked a lot of British town names but some of the homegrown ones are rather rum: Woodenbong, Black Butt, Chinaman's Knob, Dunnydoo and Tittybong.

The mayor of an Austrian village has appealed to tourists to stop stealing his road signs. Siegried Hauppl said the local council of Fucking was fed up with having to replace signs stolen as souvenirs.

It seems that the small town of Fucking has existed for over 800 years, and the locals didn't discover the English meaning until 1945, when British and American soldiers were stationed in the area.

USA

The Americans, being straight-shooting types, have two towns called Intercourse, eight Beavers, a couple of Hookers and seven Climaxes.

Bald Knob, AR
Ballville, OH
Beaver, AR
Beaver, KS
Beaver, OK
Beaver, OR

Beaver, PA
Beaver Head, ID
Beaver Lick, KY
Big Beaver, PA
Bumpass, VA
Butts, VA
Climax, CO
Climax, GA
Climax, MI
Climax, MN
Climax, NY
Climax, NC
Climax, OH
Conception, MO
Dickey, ME

Fannie, AR
Fort Dick, CA
French Lick, IN
Hooker, AR
Hooker, OK
Intercourse, AL
Intercourse, PA
Licking, MO
Love Ladies, NJ
New Beaver, PA
Peach Bottom, PA
Peach Bottom, VA
Shafter, CA
Short Pump, VA
Sweet Lips, TN

Just off Shaftesbury Avenue in London's West End, you'll find Grape Street. Nothing remarkable about this minor thoroughfare, you might think: yet way back in the thirteenth century, it went by the cheerfully upfront name of Gropecunt Lane. At that time, anyone seeking sexual favours could also try their luck in Love Lane, Maid Lane and Cock Lane.

It seems that London was not the only city that boasted a Gropecunt Lane. According to *The Guardian*, a Dr Nigel Baker confirms that you'd also have found streets with this name in York, Norwich, Oxford, Bristol, Newcastle, Southampton, Hereford, Wells, Banbury, Worcester, Shrewsbury and Reading.

And in Paris, in the fifteenth century, anyone in search of a brothel could make a beeline for Rue Poilecon (Hairy Cunt Road). Sadly, it too has since changed its name.

Deep Throat was the first hardcore sex film to cross over into the mainstream, immediately establishing itself upon its release in the US, as the must-see movie of 1972. The film is also reputed to be one of the most profitable motion pictures of all time: made for just $25,000, it's said to have have grossed in excess of $600 million to date. However, precise figures are difficult to quantify as funding and distribution of the movie was largely taken care of by the Mafia – or in this instance, the Muffia.

Despite its success, *Deep Throat* is a pretty dire film. Nevertheless, it proved to be the right porn movie at the right time, capitalising as it did on a burgeoning spirit of sexual liberation within America. And as a novel example of a movie which combined hardcore sex with a bona fide storyline – about a woman whose clit is located in the back of her throat and who can only achieve orgasm by administering blow-jobs – *Deep Throat* had audiences queuing round the block to view it. The film was actually banned in 23 states, but attempts by the authorities to suppress the film in other parts of the country only further whetted the public's appetite to see it.

Despite attaining worldwide fame and notoriety, the film's star Linda Lovelace earned just $1,200 for her sensational cock-swallowing performance, and soon afterwards her career hit the skids. She claimed in her 1980 autobiography, *Ordeal*, that she was forced at gunpoint by her husband, Chuck Traynor, to perform in *Deep Throat*. It was an allegation which was dismissed by many in the adult industry but was subsequently seized upon with glee by the feminist anti-porn movement. Lovelace's troubled life came to an untimely end in 2002 when she was killed in a car crash, aged 53. Courtney Love is set to star as Linda Lovelace in a forthcoming biopic of the porn star.

■ **Linda's co-star, Harry Reems, pocketed just $250 for his movie performance. A born-again Christian, he now lives in Salt Lake City, selling real estate.**

TURN-ONS

for women
- lycra cycling shorts
- military uniforms
- kilts
- black leather
- tight t-shirts/singlets
- erotic piercings
- sexy, kinky drag
- bare-arsed chaps
- suited and booted
- sunglasses
- butt hugging undies
- silk shirts
- totally naked

for men
- kinky boots
- strappy shoes
- sheer stockings
- basques & corsets
- exotic masks
- keeping hat on
- erotic piercings
- long gloves, Gilda-style
- fur coat, no knickers
- skimpy knicks & thongs
- wet t-shirts
- in bondage
- nekkid

WHAT'S HOT & WHAT'S NOT...

The results of a rigorously scientific poll, conducted in the pub on a Friday night

PASSION-KILLERS

for women
- cheap aftershave
- keeping socks on
- string vest & pants
- nylon football shirts
- novelity thongs
- sandals with socks
- shell suits
- toupees
- any trainers
- too much bling-bling
- indiscriminate tatts
- baggy fashion jeans
- tweed

for men
- shell suits
- lycra leotards
- loud perfume
- anoraks
- dungarees
- untamed bush
- slippers with bunnies
- pop socks
- thermal underwear
- head scarves
- flannellette pyjamas
- big baggy jumpers
- sensible shoes

BUY ME AND STOP ONE

?BC
Coitus Interruptus or, 'whipping it out before coming' is discovered. Pretty early on, someone must have noticed this did not make cavegirl Big With Child... However later found not to be 100% safe as precum can contain sperm.

1500BC
In Egypt, the first medical text is written on how to make a vaginal pessary (vaginal suppository) from crocodile dung. This is lubricated with honey or oil. To plug the cervix, women use honey and sodium bicarbonate, beeswax, or opium resin where available. The first spermicide is created using acacia tips and honey.

1000BC
The Egyptians use a linen condom to protect against disease.

100–200AD
Cave paintings at Combarelles in France show evidence of condom use in Europe.

1500s
Women discouraged to have orgasms as it is believed they decrease fertility. Syphilis epidemic across Europe. Italian anatomist Gabrielle Fallopio publishes first account of a linen sheath to protect men against syphilis.

1700s
Dr Condom gets credit for inventing the condom for Charles II to prevent the birth of more illegitimate children. The great lover Casanova praised his 'English ridingcoat' (usually made of animal intestines). For the poor, Miss Jenny sells used, washed condoms.

1800s
In France, women use half of a squeezed lemon as a cervical cap.

1843
Goodyear and Hancock discover rubber vulcanisation. It is now possible to mass produce condoms quickly and cheaply.

1873
The Comstock Law prohibits the advertising of birth control in the USA and allows the postal service to confiscate condoms sold through the US mail.

1882
The first family planning clinic opened in Holland, only to come up against fierce opposition by the medical profession,

1893
The first vasectomies are performed on human males. The unkindest cut of all, some say, but many swear by it as the healthiest option.

1909
The modern IUD is invented.

1919
In Ohio, Frederick Killian initiates hand-dipping from the longer lasting, more durable, odourless natural rubber latex.

1921
The first birth control clinic in Britain was opened in London by the brave, pioneering Marie Stopes and her husband. However Marie was a keen believer in eugenics and blotted her otherwise spotless copybook by preaching compulsory sterilisation for, among others, 'the feebleminded, revolutionaries and half-castes.' Oh dear.

1957
First lubricated condom launched in the UK by Durex.

1960
The contraceptive pill, developed in the 1950s by Gregory Pincus and funded by the US Grande Dame of Family Planning, the wealthy Katherine McCormick, first appears on the US market (as a contraceptive – a year prior to this it was only prescribed for 'menstrual disorders') in 1960. Birth control pills go on sale in Britain the following year.

1968
Pope Paul VI, flying in the face of the Papal commission on birth control, tells the world's Catholics that the only method of contraception open to them is 'Vatican Roulette', ie the rhythm method. Effectively this bans condoms which in turn helps to spread STDs in developing countries. This encyclical, ironically entitled 'Of Human Life', endorsed by subsequent popes, later condemns to death many Catholic Africans during the (ongoing) Aids crisis. Never has the suggestion 'you no playa da game, you no maka da rules' made more sense.

1970
Use of condoms as a contraceptive device decline as the pill, the coil and sterilisation become more popular.

1980s
Condom use increases strikingly following the recognition of HIV/Aids, but the estimated number of women on the pill is 50–80 million world-wide.

1990s
Flavoured and coloured condoms introduced. The female condom available in Europe and the US.

1994
The first polyurethane condom for men launched in the US.

2005
We are still waiting for the 'Male Pill' to appear on the market. One of the avenues of male chemical contraception being investigated is a pill that would cause sperm to lose their tails or flagellae, thereby inhibiting any wanderlust on their part. Poor things.

This A-Z is intended as an overview of some of the things that folk get up to in the name of sex. Some other interesting sex practices are covered elsewhere in this book.

And we've not included many of the more outlandish and bizarre 'paraphilias', such as dendrophilia (sexual arousal from trees); or taphephilia (arousal gained from being buried alive) as this is probably a once-only thrill!

Adult Babies

Infantilism is the term applied to fetishists who achieve arousal through adopting the characteristics of a baby or infant. Infantilists will source and wear oversized baby clothing such as bonnets, bibs and baby-grows and will usually identify with a maternal participant, who assumes the role of mother or nanny during 'adult baby' sessions.

Animal Training

Animal training refers to erotic play which involves dressing and adopting the persona and traits of a specific animal, often with a 'trainer' attached. In 'pony play', for instance, one partner adopts the traits of a horse, while training involves them submitting to the will of the groom. Play sessions may include use of specially designed equipment such as bits, harnesses and butt-plug tails. Other animal personae such as dogs are also popular, whereby those adopting the role will eat and drink from a bowl and wear a collar and leash. *Woof!*

Blood Sports

Bloodplay involves cutting the flesh of a partner and ingesting the blood vampire-style, or practising sexual intercourse and cunnilingus during menstruation (Hell's Angels are said to earn their 'red wings' by going down on a woman at this time). Those who use blood within the context of sexual activity often testify to an increased and intense eroticism.

Body Modification
Body modification is the art of changing one's natural appearance for pleasure or sexual enhancement. Circumcision is perhaps the oldest and most common form of such modification, but other examples range from piercing and breast enlargement to far more extreme alterations such as scarification, branding, suturing and bifurcation (the splitting the shaft of the penis – ouch!).

BDSM

BDSM is a relatively new acronym, originating in the USA, encompassing several broadly related practices: bondage and discipline, domination and submission and sadomasochism.

Bondage

Essentially the act of restricting movement for sexual pleasure, rope is perhaps the most popular bondage implement, but other materials used for erotic restraint include ribbon, silk scarves, handcuffs, shackles and chains. Often the symbolism of such items have strong resonances of enslavement. A person may also be bound to open the legs and expose the genitals, whilst preventing movement during sexual activity or corporal punishment. Some find bondage removes the need for them to perform sexually without feeling guilty about enjoying the sensations, whilst for others, being unable to reciprocate reinforces their submissive role.

Breath Play

Choking and strangulation serves to limit the intake of oxygen, so intensifying sexual arousal. It also applies pressure to the carotid artery, which can also induce euphoria. However, though reducing levels of oxygen intake ►

can heighten orgasmic intensity, it can also make you drowsy and seriously affect your judgement, often with fatal consequences, particularly when it comes to the practice of auto-erotic asphyxiation.

Corporal Punishment

Corporal punishment (CP) combines a strong element of humiliation with the hitting or striking of one's submissive partner. Spanking as an intimate sexual discipline aims to produce pleasurable sensations for the submissive, and/or arousal for the dominant administering it. CP may utilise a whole array of implements such as paddles, canes, floggers and tawses, to deliver everything from a soft stroke to a stinging lash capable of drawing blood. During the ancient Greek festival of

Aphrodite, women used flagellation to build their passions for orgies, and many religious sects down the centuries have used it as a means of 'self-mortification'. Oddly, spanking and flagellation are known abroad as *le vice Anglais*.

Cross-dressing

Cross-dressing is far more prevalent amongst men than women. However, not all men who dress up as women do so for the same reasons. Though the terms are commonly confused, transvestism refers to those who gain sexual pleasure from dressing up as a women and should not be confused with drag, which is a form of cabaret involving 'female impersonators'.

Depilation

Depilation is the removal of body hair, which has been practised for many centuries. Pubic hair removal, in particular, is more popular amongst women than it is men, possibly because of the potency of the symbolism which accompanies its disappearance. For example, shorn female genitals, exposed and on show, can be taken to represent the removal of the fig leaf or the peeling away of the final veil. And the coming together of two sets of shaved genitals can introduce 'frictionless' sensations into sex as well as an added sense of physical closeness.

Dogging

'Dogging' is the term used to describe scenarios where exhibitionists have sex in remote car parks whilst being observed by voyeuristic males. The term is said to have originated in the early-Seventies to describe men who spied on couples having nookie out of doors, 'dogging' their every move in an effort to watch them screw.

Electro Stimulation

By applying a properly targeted electrical signal, the body's nerves can be activated causing different levels of sensation. Electro-sex toys such as PES boxes and violet wands are designed specifically to stimulate the genitalia with a low-voltage electrical current, producing pleasurable sexual sensations that range from a slight tingle to a throbbing pulse.

Dominance & Submission

Although closely related to sadomasochism, sub/dom differs because it is more specifically to do with the psychological thrill of exercising or renouncing power – the power exchange – rather than physical stimulation and the giving and receiving of pain. That said, sub/dom play may also incorporate these elements.

Enemas

The enema is an ancient health practice which has been adopted by modern-day fetishists. In a sexual context, enemas are used to cleanse the rectum before anal sex and as part of BDSM roleplay involving staged medical scenarios between doctor/nurse and patient. For some, the sensation of the liquid entering the body through the anus is a form of sexual stimulation in ▶

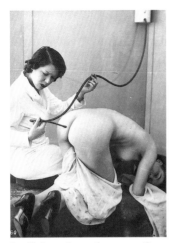

itself. For others, the evacuation of the liquid provides intense arousal. Perhaps the current fad for colonic irrigation, ostensibly for health reasons, also has its intrinsic erotic pleasures.

Exhibitionism

Exhibitionists gain arousal through exposing themselves or their sexual antics to an unsuspecting audience, thus revelling in a shocked reaction. The most recognised form of exhibitionism is the flashing male, but many women also engage in far more surreptitious acts of 'accidental' exhibitionism, for instance by bending over to pick something up in a short skirt or a low-cut top. For exhibitionistic couples, 'dogging' sites and swingers clubs provide the chance to show off and perform in front in front of an eager, appreciative audience.

Fat

The playful term 'chubby chaser' or FA (fat admirer) is applied to someone who is sexually aroused by an obese partner. Chubby chasers like to luxuriate in the soft abundance of their partner's flesh, and sometimes the relationship can develop into one of 'feeder' and 'feedee'. For a feeder, the act of literally feeding an obese partner provides sexual stimulus, whilst for a feedee, the act of being fed or fattened-up is equally as arousing.

Fisting

Fisting involves the insertion of the entire hand into the vagina or anus. Anal fisting has long been popular amongst gay men and likewise a lot of information on vaginal fisting reflects its popularity amongst lesbians. However, fisting is increasing being enjoyed by heterosexuals with many new converts attesting to powerful orgasms accompanied by ejaculation due to the pressure of the the fist directly on the G-spot.

Frottage

This is the act of rubbing one's body against another for sexual stimulation. This can be through consensual foreplay between partners (dry humping), or a non-consensual act where the frottaphile will rub up against someone else on a crowded bus or tube train, whilst pretending it was an accident if confronted.

Fetishism

The classic definition of fetishism is the attachment of an important sexual significance to an object which is not necessarily directly sexual in itself, particularly articles of clothing, such as shoes or stockings, and specific parts of the body, such as feet.

Gangbang

Group sex that is quite distinct from the classic orgy situation which involves numbers of folk having sex simultaneously, the classic definition of gangbang is 'an instance of sexual intercourse between one woman and several men, one after the other.' But though the dictionary adds 'especially against her will,' gangbangs are invariably consensual and highly-organised affairs.

Humiliation

Humiliation is commonly used between a dominant and a submissive, where both parties have negotiated and consented beforehand. Methods can range from light verbal chastisement to the submissive being forced to reveal themselves naked in public and perform menial tasks, such as serving drinks at a party. Being 'forced' to endure acts involving faeces and urine, or being made to watch one's object of desire engage in sex with another partner are also all common humiliation scenarios. The professional dominatrix makes commercial use of this desire, often using roleplay to humiliate. A common fantasy scenario ▶

33 KINKS, FETISHES & PERVY DIVERSIONS

involves the dominatrix 'forcing' the male sub to dress and adopt the persona of a young girl, then participate in 'potty training' and etiquette classes.

Knicker wetting

Knicker wetting aficionados become aroused either by observing or partaking in 'wet' or 'piss sex', which is precipitated by intentional urination, often in public. Underwear is worn, which darkens as the flow of the warm fluid spreads across the fabric. Part of the appeal is to do with the increasing discomfort of holding the urine in, which in turn heightens the relief of emptying the bladder; and with the attendant shame of the woman 'losing control', particularly if it occurs in public.

Medical

Medical-fetish devotees are coming out of the cubicle: enemas and stainless steel dildos are now in vogue. The primary arousal factor for some medical-fetishists is the roleplay scenario: a desire to recreate childhood games of doctors and nurses. For others it is the medical acts which provide the most arousal. The doctor or nurse relishes the chance to examine the 'patient' who is often cleaned of his or her body fluids and faecal matter. Equipment used in medical scenes invariably includes furniture and implements found in a regular doctor's surgery, especially those used for gynaecological and rectal examinations.

Mummification

Used by ancient cultures to preserve the dead, modern mummification is now used in BDSM sex play as a form of bondage. The 'mummy' is wrapped from feet to the neck with either bandages, cling film or PVC bondage tape, often leaving the genitals, anus and breasts exposed allowing them to freely stimulate the erogenous zones of the bound captive. By removing the ability to move and adding a blindfold the stimulus concentrated on the exposed area of the skin becomes intensified and more sensitive. In extreme mummification, the whole body and head can be totally encased.

Plushies & Furries

A 'furry' is a person who becomes sexually aroused when adopting the persona, sexual traits and furry costume of a particular animal that excites them. Plushies, meanwhile, enjoy sexual relations with specially-made animal toys which have been modified so they can be rubbed up against, or inserted in the vagina, for masturbation. Did Walt Disney ever imagine it would come to this?

Queening

The term 'queening' refers to the act whereby a female sits on a male's head or face, using it as her 'throne', often leading to cunnilingus and rimming. The venerable tradition of face-sitting has a long history: in Elizabethan times, male servants would often be required to provide a certain kind of 'lip service' whilst buried beneath their ladies' skirts. And apparently, the ancient Persians created special chairs with a hole in the middle where a man could place his face whilst his partner took the weight off her feet. Queening can be put to good use in humiliation scenarios, where the female smothers the male's nose and mouth with her buttocks and clenched thighs. Here, the object is physical restraint and breath control, too. Queening may also include farting; in which case, the 'queen' will break wind on her subject's face.

Roleplay

Roleplay is effectively a form of erotic make-believe in which the participants act out erotic personae within passion plays of ▶

their own devising. Typical roleplays include the prostitute and her client, the French maid and the abusive master of the house, the lap-dancer and her captivated audience, the teacher and the pupil and even fictional super-heroes; 'You saved my life, Superman – how can I ever repay you?' Roleplay allows us to enact sexual situations in the bedroom, which might be unattainable in the outside world, such as abduction and rape fantasies.

Ultimately, the beauty of roleplay is that you are limited only by your imagination.

Sadomasochism

Sadism is 'the gaining of pleasure or sexual gratification from the infliction of pain and mental suffering on another person'; while masochism is the gaining of pleasure or sexual gratification from receiving pain. Unsurprisingly the two are often regarded as closely connected.

The term 'masochism' was named after the writer, Leopold von Sacher Masoch and 'sadism' after the infamous French libertine, the Marquis de Sade, whose novels described non-consensual acts of gratuitous sexual sadism. These days we tend to view the sadist within the context of sadomasochistic relationships, where the pain and suffering inflicted is consented to by the masochist. The skill of the sadist is to know how to vary the pain inflicted to maximise the attendant pleasure alongside the pain. The skill of the masochist is knowing how far to allow it to go. In many cases, when a dom and a sub get it on, it's a match made in heaven!

Shoe & Foot Worship

Foot worship is the term used to describe the practices of kissing, stroking, sniffing, licking or sucking toes and feet to achieve sexual arousal. Tastes amongst foot lovers (who are almost always men) vary, with some liking the foot to be bare and others preferring stockinged feet. Foot worship is closely linked to shoe fetishism, with many podophiliacs deriving pleasure from the sight of feet shod in high heels.

Suction/Cupping/Pumping

Suction is the key principle in 'cupping' where small cup-like devices are placed on the surface of the skin. The air is then removed which creates the suction which in turn causes blood to flow to the surface, so increasing sensitivity. When used on the nipples and labia, cupping causes them to swell, and for many, it is the sight of the extremely engorged genitals that provides the attraction.

Voyeurism

Voyeurism is a very common kink which runs the whole gamut from watching pornography and visiting peepshows, to spying on your neighbours *in flagrante*. For most people, a little peeking is just one manifestation of a general interest in sex. For some though, arousal comes only from watching others having sex, as opposed to doing it themselves. In this respect, exhibitionists, who become aroused through performing to an audience are to voyeurs what sadists are to masochists. Exhibitionistic couples frequently advertise in contact magazines for voyeurs to watch them while they have sex.

Watersports

Absolutely nothing to do with surfing or being pulled on skis behind a speedboat, this is the practice of peeing on your partner or being peed on, known as 'golden showers'. It also may involve watching your partner urinate. The urine may be drunk or projected onto the partner's face, genitals and body. Golden showers can also be administered as a form of 'punishment' or humiliation during sub/dom play, but many enthusiasts simply enjoy watersports play mutually as an intimate experience in its own right.

PORN BARONS

From fairly humble beginnings, they made their fortunes in porno, and now figure in the Sunday Times *'Rich List', each with wealth estimated in excess of £500million. Read and learn...*

Richard Desmond Prior to becoming proprietor of the *Express* and *Star* newspapers and *OK!* magazine, Desmond published top-shelf men's magazines, which he recently relinquished, though he still owns a number of soft porn TV channels. His company Northern & Shell is privately owned, and he is estimated to be worth £1.3billion.

David Sullivan Perhaps best known for his *Sunday Sport* paper, Sullivan has had interests in most areas of the adult industry over the past thirty years. He claims to have slept with 15,000 women, commenting: 'What's the point of owning the sweetie shop and not eating the sweets?' He has since sold his magazine portfolio to the Gold brothers, but remains co-owner of Birmingham City FC.

Paul Raymond Back in 1957, he opened Raymond's Revuebar in Soho, London and the glamorous nude stage shows proved an immediate success. In 1971, Raymond turned to magazine publishing with the launch of a string of girlie mags such as *Men Only* and *Club International*. His daughter, Debbie, who was to have taken over the reins of the company in the 90s, died of a drug overdose and Raymond grew increasingly reclusive, but retains substantial property interests in Soho.

David, Ralph & Jacqui Gold With Goldstar Publications, brothers David and Ralph Gold accumulated considerable wealth with a number of top-shelf titles and other adult interests. David's daughter, Jacqui (pictured), heads up Ann Summers, with its long-established party plan business (a sexed-up variation of Tupperware parties for women only) and a chain of high-street adult shops.

ROGUES, RAKES & ROUÉS

Giles de Rais

Gosh, this man really was an out-and-out bounder, even though he saved France, was the prototype for Bluebeard and must have made brilliant copy for the Marquis de Sade. Gilles De Rais (1404-1440) tortured and killed hundreds of children for his own sexual pleasure in a variety of sickening ways. Until brought to book for his evil crimes, he was considered a hero: rich, handsome, aristocratic and France's top general in the Hundred Years War. Devil worship, human sacrifice and sodomy were just three of the 47 charges brought against him at his trial, which ended in a sentence of death by strangulation.

Earl of Rochester

John Wilmot, Earl of Rochester (1647-1680) was given an Oxford degree at the age of 14. Aged 18, he tried, unsuccessfully, to abduct Elizabeth Malet ('the great beauty and fortune of the North' as Pepys noted), then married her two years later. He and his aristocratic co-rakes formed The Merry Gang, a group notorious for their drunken, bawdy revelries. As well as some conventional poetry that rivalled the works of Marvell

and Donne, he is remembered for writing the obscene play *Sodom*, as well as numerous poems and satires in the same vein, including one on his monarch, which begins:

> *In th' isle of Britain, long since famous grown*
> *For breeding the best cunts in Christendom,*
> *There reigns, and oh! long may he reign and thrive,*

The easiest King and best bred man alive.

Charles II banned him from Court and Rochester took up as 'Dr Bendo', a consultant in barrenness, apparently with considerable success. He died of syphilis, aged 33.

The Marquis de Sade

The Marquis de Sade (1740-1814) would definitely be deemed 'unsafe in taxis' by mothers of today, as he was in his own time. All the same, the image of a rampaging, heartless, homicidal aristocrat of the sort that gave the guillotine a good name, is a tad misleading. He was henpecked and harried by his mother-in-law, never murdered anyone and loved to give swinging parties which were necessarily populated with riffraff and prostitutes.

Eventually things got out of hand, and after injudicious use of dodgy aphrodisiacs he was hauled up on charges of attempted murder and 'unnatural acts', thus beginning a long series of incarcerations. De Sade spent much of his adult life in prisons or institutions where to allay boredom he wrote sexually graphic novels (*Justine, Juliette, 120 Days of Sodom*) and philosophical plays:

O voluptuous young women, deliver your bodies unto us as often and as much as you wish!
Fuck, divert yourselves, that's the essential thing;
but be quick to fly from love.

In these he catalogued the worst human excesses and sexual fetishes his imagination could furnish, giving rise to the term 'sadism' and pre-empting Krafft Ebing's *Psychopathia Sexualis* by 100 years. His final imprisonment at Charenton inspired the thought-provoking play and the movie *Quills*, starring Geoffrey Rush and Kate Winslett.

Sir Francis Dashwood

At his High Wycombe family estate, Sir Francis Dashwood (1708-1781) ran the Cliveden (Lord Astor, Christine Keeler, John Profumo) of his day, where Establishment sin and sex mingled with politics and intrigue. The Hell Fire Club started at Medmenham Abbey which Sir Francis had purchased and turned into an erotic theme park. Hell Fire club members took part in fake religious ceremonies with masks and costumes that permitted acts of incognito debauchery. When this location became too notorious, the club moved to a more secluded site at West Wycombe caves. Other members of the club included the Earl of Sandwich, Thomas Potter (the son of the Archbishop of Canterbury), John Wilkes, William Hogarth, the Earl of Bute, the Marquis of Granby, the Prince of Wales and possibly Benjamin Franklin and Horace Walpole. Some say the 'monks' took prostitutes down the Thames from London in barges to act as lewd 'nuns'. There were accusations of celebrating the Black Mass over the naked bodies of upper-class ladies, one of whom was Lady Mary Montagu Wortley, the mother-in-law of the Earl of Bute. Motto: *Fay ce que voudres* (Do whatever you will).

Aleister Crowley

Named by the 1920s tabloids as 'The Wickedest Man in the World', Aleister Crowley (1875-1947), aka 'The Beast', always seemed to court notoriety. That being said, he was a bright lad: British chess master, mountain climber, poet, writer, painter, social critic, occultist, mystic, astrologer and sexual revolutionary. Believing himself to be the messiah of a new era, he pursued his first serious experiments in sex magick, convinced that any form of sexual activity was good in itself. This led to rituals involving multiple male and female partners, and when he moved to Sicily with a new lover, stories of depraved sexual activities quickly began to emanate from the island.

Most roués would have been content with inheriting a brewery, as he did, but oh no, Aleister had to go and squander it all on being as bad and spooky as he could, writing crap books about the occult (much loved by ageing rockers) and ending up dying a junkie in a Brighton boarding house.

21 THINGS XXX MOVIES TAUGHT US ABOUT SEX

Women never have headaches or periods.

Attractive women enjoy having sex with ugly middle-aged men.

Men don't have to beg.

Men are never ever impotent.

Women wear high heels to bed.

Men always groan 'Oh yeah!' when they come.

Women always look pleasantly surprised when they open a man's trousers and find a dick there.

Women moan uncontrollably when giving a blow job.

All women are noisy shags.

Men always pull out.

Women always orgasm when men do.

Double penetration makes women smile.

Women also smile appreciatively when men splat them in the face with semen.

When going down on a woman, ten seconds is more than satisfactory.

A common, enjoyable sex practice for a man is to take his semi-erect penis and slap it repeatedly on a woman's backside.

A man ejaculating over a woman's bum is a satisfying result for all parties concerned.

Lubricants are unnecessary, even during long bouts of anal sex. A little saliva is quite enough.

If a woman is caught masturbating by a strange man, she won't scream with embarrassment, but rather insist he have sex with her right there and then.

If you come across a couple having sex, the boyfriend won't bash you up if you shove your dick in his girlfriend's mouth.

People in the Eighties couldn't fuck unless there was a sax solo in the background.

When standing during a blow job, a man will always place one hand firmly on the back of the kneeling woman's head and the other proudly on his hip.

THE HARD SELL

It has been officially available on prescription in this country for just over five years now, and despite a drop in demand after the initial clamour, **Viagra** continues to be the most demanded of all drugs: worldwide sales of the little blue pill totalled around £1billion last year – a figure which doesn't take into account sales on the grey market. And a quick search for Viagra on the web will net you five million results. Viagra is also commonly used by male porn performers to keep their peckers up during prolonged filming, though few will admit it! Oh, and did you know that government figures reveal that people in the London Borough of Islington consumed more Viagra than anywhere else in the country!

■ *Viagra was recently compared by one wag to a Disneyland ride. Well, they're both expensive; you then have to wait for about an hour for a three-minute ride; and they often leave you feeling a bit sick afterwards...*

Stiff Competition

These days, there is a number of new impotence cures. For starters, there's Cialis. It's known as Le Weekend in France due to its considerably longer-lasting effects — up to 24 hours or more, as opposed to around five hours for Viagra. The advantage of this extended time period is that it restores a welcome degree of spontaneity. Then there's Levitra, which is comparable to Viagra in that it acts for a similar duration of time, but the effects come on more quickly. Also, it has less potential for adverse reactions to food and drink.

Other such drugs include Uprima (which may help with psychological difficulties relating to impotence), Yohimbine Hydrochloride and Carbergoline. Melatonin is a prescription-only remedy for jet-lag, but a version which specifically targets the sexual receptors is expected soon, in the form of a nasal spray.

Lolo Ferrari was the embodiment of anatomical excess. Born Eve Vallois, her professional name of Lolo was taken from the French slang for breasts, *les lolos*. This name became particularly appropriate as Ferrari eventually underwent nineteen (!) breast 'enhancement' operations throughout the 1990s, and earned herself a place in the *Guinness Book of Records* for her gargantuan 54G boobs, which weighed in at three kilos each.

Some people just don't know when to stop. Having appeared in a couple of hardcore films, Lolo, together with her manager and husband, Eric Vigne, quickly discovered that the bigger her chest became, the more work came her way. However, there was a heavy price to pay in the form of subsequent physical restrictions.

By 1997 Lolo was reportedly reluctant to take a flight to London for fear that changes in air pressure might cause her breasts to explode. That aside, we can only speculate upon the damage that life – quite literally as a standing joke and a cheap laugh on such TV shows as *Eurotrash* – exacted upon the self-esteem of a woman who, by all accounts, was intelligent. Although the coroner's verdict was natural causes, the suggestion made in many quarters was that Lolo committed suicide.

TREASURE CHESTS

TREASURE CHESTS

Britain's own Cathy Barry, **sex celebrity, adult TV presenter and porn star, can now claim to have the largest pair of boobs in the country. To achieve her record-busting 34JJJ boobs, Cathy has undergone a total of six breast implant procedures (one of which was filmed live on Channel Five in 2005).**

And now, Turner Prize-winning artist, Gillian Wearing, has created a lifecast of her face and torso, which is scheduled to be exhibited at Tate Modern.

Booby Prize A breast implant belonging to Tawny Peaks, a former stripper and *Playboy* cover model, was auctioned on eBay in 2005 and went on to fetch around £10,000.

Ms Peaks' 69HH-size peaks first made news back in 1998 when she was accused of assaulting a man at a stag party with her mega-mammaries. The victim claimed to have suffered whiplash injury after he was smacked in the chops by her bouncing boobs. Despite the claimant's statement that they were 'like two cement blocks', the People's Court dismissed the claim.

A year later, Tawny's tits were restored to something approaching normality when she had the implants removed. And recently, when she discovered her bosom boosters stashed away in a box, she decided to sell one (but keep the other for old times' sake).

On eBay, the auction for the single, signed implant finally closed when Golden Palace Casino – which has a reputation for acquiring bizarre memorabilia – bid nearly $17,000.

LONG JOHN HOLMES

Perhaps the most famous male porn star of all time, John Holmes was reputedly the most well-endowed, with thirteen inches of love muscle when erect; though his ex-wife recalled him to be ten inches in length and four inches in circumference – still, not to be sniffed at.

Appropriately nicknamed Johnny Wadd, Holmes starred in some 2,000 hardcore films during a lengthy career which stretched from the late Sixties to the early Eighties. He is reported to have screwed many hundreds of women, including all of the top stars of the day, such as Seka, Linda Lovelace, Marilyn Chambers and La Cicciolina.

During the late-Seventies, Holmes became increasingly dependent on cocaine which severely impaired his ability to rise to the occasion, and he subsequently turned to crime to maintain his habit. In 1982, he was implicated and eventually acquitted of involvement in a notoriously brutal, drug-related multiple murder, which was the subject of the 2004 film *Wonderland* (starring Val Kilmer). Johnny Wadd was also said to be the inspiration behind the Dirk Diggler character in the film *Boogie Nights*.

Holmes, who also appeared in numerous gay movies, was diagnosed HIV-positive in 1986, but was said to have continued to make films without informing any of his partners (what a guy!). He eventually succumbed to Aids and died on 13 March 1988, aged 43.

SEX DOT COM-EDY

the tangled web of sex.com

We all know that sex is the biggest thing on the internet, and in 1994, a Mr Gary Kremen of San Francisco had the foresight to register the domain name, sex.com – potentially an enormously lucrative move. But he chose not to do anything with the name for the time being.

In the meantime, gangster Stephen Cohen was released from prison, following a stretch for impersonating a bankruptcy lawyer. He, too, had the idea of registering sex.com. When he discovered that it belonged to somebody else, his enthusiasm for his project remained undaunted: he simply forged a letter of transfer, saying that Kremen no longer required the domain name and sent it to Network Solutions, with whom it was registered. The plan worked, and Cohen then turned sex. com into the profitable porn portal that you would expect – reputedly raking in monthly revenues of $500,000.

That was until November 2000, when a court awarded Kremen the return of the domain name, having discovered that the forged signature on the letter to Network Solutions misspelled the name of the purported signatory, giving the game away nicely. Cohen was ordered to pay the hefty sum of $65 million in damages. Instead of coughing up, he fled the country, and despite Kremen offering a $50,000 bounty for his capture, Cohen has not been found and was apparently last sighted in Tijuana, Mexico.

Kremen, meanwhile, supports himself on his share of sex.com's monthly revenues – now a mere $300,000 a month!

A LEXICON OF **LUST**

anal intercourse buggery, go Hollywood, goose, Greek, Russian wrestling, sodomy, butt slamming, reaming, bum fuck, backscuttle, turd burgling

anus back passage, bunghole, chocolate starfish, hole, Elephant and Castle, stinkhole bay, rectum, ring, wrong door, arsehole, cornhole, poop chute, rosebud, brown eye, wazoo, backdoor

analingus brown nose, eating ass, *feuille de rose*, postillonage, rimming, ring around the moon, tongue in the hairy, tossing salad, arse-licking

bestiality barnyard lover, bring your own licker, chicken fucker, (kanga) 'roo rooting, sheep dip, wellington boots,

bisexual AC/DC, bats for both teams, bi, switch hitter, double adaptor

breasts boobies, bazongas, cabman's rests, cans, cat and kitties, cherrylets, headlights, jugs, kettle drums, knockers, melons, ta-tas, titties, bristols

buttocks ass, bum, fanny, fife and drum, flesh cushions, haunches, keister, rear, rump, tuchus, Turkish beauties, arse, booty

circumcised acorn, brissed, cut, kosher, Nova Scotia, roundhead, Woolworth's clip, clipped

clitoris button, clit, ecstasy switch, pink bud, peeping sentinel, man in a boat, pearl

condom connies, English ridingcoat, French letter, mac, johnny, rubber

penis (rhyming slang: good ship Venus); bald-headed hermit, bean, bone, cock (rhyming slang: almond [rock], dickory dock, grandfather clock, padlock, stick of rock); chopper (rhyming slang: gobstopper); corie (rhyming slang: gruesome and gory); dick (rhyming slang: Hampton Wick), John, pecker, pego, peter, percy, rod, schlong, trouser snake, todger, wang, willy, prick, tool, John Thomas, manhood

cunnilingus carpet munching, drinking from the fur cup,

eating out, going down, honey-potting, lunching at the Y, muff-diving, parting the marinated beef curtains, tonguing, sneezing in the cabbage, pearl diving, box lunch, yodelling in the canyon

ejaculate blow your wad, come, haul your ashes, put in the boot, shoot your load, slime, spend

erection angle of dangle, blue veiner, boner, crack a fat, hard-on, loaded gun, packing heat, rampant Hampton, salute, stiffy

fellatio BJ, blow job, deep throat, give head, pompe, play the magic flute, suck cock, gob-job, gnaw the 'nana, gobble

female genitals beaver, cock alley (also cock chafer, cock hall, cock-holder, cock inn, cock lane, cock locker, cock pit, cockshire), cunt (rhyming slang: all quiet, gasp and grunt, sharp and blunt, Berkley Hunt, treasure hunt), cunny, clit, crack, cupid's highway, fanny, fitz, fur burger, fur cup, jelly roll, glue factory, hole, love box, minge, mystic grotto, oyster, pit, prick-holder, prick purse, punani, poontang, pussy, rubyfruit jungle, snatch, twat, quim, slit, gash

to have sex from behind doggy style, *en levrette*, like a lioness on a cheese scraper, up in the hat rack

lesbian butch, carpet muncher, dyke, fanny tickler, finger artist, harpy, lezzie, quim queer, clithopper

homosexual ass bandit, donut puncher, fairy, fudge packer, gay, haricot, homo, limp wrist, poofter, possodeluxe, queen, turd burglar, colon commando, knob jockey

kiss frenching, peck, snog, suck face, tonsil hockey, swap spit

masturbate bash the bishop, beat the meat, choke the chicken, diddle yourself, engaging sixth gear, finger fuck, five-knuckle shuffle, flog your dolphin, jack off, jerkin the gherkin, Levy and Frank, Mrs Palm and her five daughters, J Arthur Rank, stroke it, married to the five-fingered widow, toss one off, twang the wang, varnish the ▶

cane, wank, polish the pearl, jill off, tweak the clit

nipples cherries, half inch bolts, nips, rosebuds, ruby jewels, teats

orgasm banners and drums, big O, come, get off, *le petit mort*, climax

orgy daisy chain, group sex, lifestyles, partouse, Roman, soft swing, cluster fuck

pubic hair bush, bushy park, hairy Mary, hair pie, jungle, kitten's ear, map of Tasmania, muff, sewer bushes, short and curlies, snatch, thatch

scrotum ball bag, codlings, lust cluster, Mephistopholes purse, nut sack, wrinkled retainer

semen baby juice, cum, cream, jism, jizz, jollies, load, love juice, smeddum, spunk, seed

sexual intercourse ball bashing, bonking, bumping uglies, empty the bag, fuck, get your kettle mended, sow your oats, hump, jump her/his bones, make whoopee, making the two backed beast, nail, nookie, pizzle, pluggin' the spear in the bearded clam, prick the garter, screw, squelching, take a turn on Mount Pleasant, shagging, horizontal jogging, rumpy-pumpy

sixty-nine boating, nose to tail, *tête bêche*, *soixante-neuf*, 71 minus 2

testicles balls (rhyming slang: Henry Halls, marble halls, Niagra Falls, Max Walls, etc); bollocks (rhyming slang: fun and frolics, Jackson Pollocks); cojones, family jewels, flowers and frolics, goolies, huevos, leerodies, nuts, spunkholders, twiddlediddles, knackers, cobblers (rhyming slang: cobblers' awls)

swinging wife swapping, key games, trade off, 2+2, polyamory, open marriage

threesome *la main officieuse, menage à trois*, sex sandwich, three-way, twos-up

transsexual the big surprise, go to Denmark, he-she, Swedish number, teddy bear's picnic

transvestite butterfly in moth's clothing, cross-dresser, gender-bender, TV

urolagnia golden showers, piss games, watersports

BOOM GANG-A-BANG

It may not appear in the *Guinness Book of Records*, but attempts at setting the record for the world's biggest gangbang are always likely to generate more interest than those for stuffing marbles up the nose.

The concept was famously created by 22-year-old Annabel Chong, who in 1995 earned herself a place in the pantheon of porn, by sucking and fucking 251 men in ten hours. She briefly became the most

famous porn star on earth with the video of the event going on to become the biggest selling in American XXX history (although Chong never made a penny from it). A revealing documentary, *Sex*, was made charting the ups and downs of this most unlikely of sex stars, in the two years following her sex-a-thon. Chong comes across as a rather naive gender-studies undergraduate, rebelling against her stifling middle-class upbringing in Singapore. She may have been attempting to make a point about the voraciousness of female sexuality but, as she finds to her cost, a star's only as big as her last gangbang.

Chong's achievement was swiftly eclipsed by stripper Jasmin St Claire, leaving her only with the kudos of having been the first. Subsequent scores have been racked up on the fuck-o-meter including US porn star Houston's 620 men.

In Poland, a three-pronged attempt was made at surpassing even Houston's total. So, in the first Annual Gangbang Championship in Warsaw, three competitors, Claire Brown from the UK, Mayara from Brazil and local girl, Klaudia Figura, attempted to set a new record. British hopes were dashed when Claire Brown dropped out after a mere 466 penetrations. Klaudia Figura went on to beat the Brazilian into second place, and succeeded in setting a new world gangbang record, after being humped 646 times. Crikey... that's six litres of semen expended!

MWAH! MWAH! MWAH!

While the evolutionary origins of the kiss remain unknown, we're quite taken by the actress Ingmar Bergman's explanation that, 'A kiss is a lovely trick designed by nature to stop speech when words become superfluous.'

The world kissing record was broken in July 2005 by a British couple, James Belshaw and Sophie Severin, who snogged continuously for 31 hours, 30 minutes and 30 seconds at the Plaza Shopping Centre, London. Following the setting of the previous record by an Italian couple, the male kisser had to be resuscitated by oxygen.

In an average lifetime, a person spends about two weeks locking lips and tangling tongues. Apparently, during an especially passionate kiss, you can burn two calories a minute.

Scientific trials have discovered that a man's saliva fills with the male hormone testosterone, upon seeing an attractive woman. Kissing passes some of those hormones on to the female, making her more in the mood for love.

The first cinematic kiss was a middle-aged snog between John C Rice and his screen partner May Irwin in a 1896 film, appropriately called *The Kiss*. The longest kiss on celluloid – three-and-a-half minutes – was between Jane Wyman and Ray Tooney in the 1941 film, *You're in the Army Now*. Actor John Barrymore holds the record for the number of screen kisses in a movie, smooching his female co-stars 127 times during *Don Juan* in 1926.

Clark Gable may have been one of the most famous of screen kissers, but his co-star in *Gone With the Wind*, Vivien Leigh, is said to have complained about his halitosis. Conversely,

Diana Rigg reportedly chewed raw garlic to discourage George Lazenby from getting too enthusiastic in the love scenes during the making of *On Her Majesty's Secret Service*.

The Roman Emperor Tiberius issued a decree banning kissing, because it was believed to be responsible for the spread of mentagra, an unpleasant fungal disease which disfigured the faces of Roman nobles.

The world record for the number of simultaneous kisses was broken on Valentine's Day 2004, when 5,122 Filipino couples locked lips for the required 10 seconds. This beat the previous record set the year before by 4,500 Chilean couples.

WEIRD WORLD OF SEX #5

Officer Officer: 'We couldn't possibly comment on what an officer does in his spare time,' was the official line taken by police in Stone, Staffordshire, following an embarrassing incident which left one of their number in need of cosmetic surgery. Having returned home from a night shift, an unnamed police officer began making lustful advances towards his wife as she made a sizzling breakfast of sausages and bacon.

Seeking to prepare a deliciously mouth-watering treat for her in return, the man proceeded to wrap a slice of bread around his penis. Unfortunately instead of igniting his wife's passions, the man's meat became minced morsels as the couple's salivating pet labrador leapt to claim his prize. Following a struggle punctuated by bloodcurdling screams, the hungry hound eventually relinquished its grip, leaving the bobby writhing in agony with his hot-dog distinctly heavy on the ketchup.

CINDERELLA COURTESANS

These lowborn lasses who shagged above their station were neither 'common' prostitutes nor kept mistresses.

Christine Keeler

Possibly the last lady who could have been considered a courtesan, and whose role in the shagathon that eventually brought a government to its knees, was Christine Keeler. It was 1963, in the Cold War-era, when Keeler's torrid affairs with both John Profumo (Secretary of State for War) and a Russian diplomat caused a news frenzy. Lurid tales of orgies in stately homes, and skinny-dipping aristos filled the press for months on end and made Keeler, and her friend Mandy Rice-Davis, infamous.

Described as a model, but seen as a harlot at the time, Keeler retreated into silence and has only recently raised her head above the parapet. Lewis Morley's photograph of the naked Keeler straddling a chair became an icon of 1960s Britain and can be seen in the National Portrait Gallery.

Nell Gwynne

When you think of courtesans, the first name that springs to mind is often Nell Gwynne, mistress of King Charles ll. Nell was, in fact, an actress, though at the time all actresses were regarded by polite society as 'brazen and tarred' women. So Nell decided to live up to the title, calling herself The Protestant Whore, and behaving in a wild and indiscreet manner, as well as mixing it with anti-French politics, much to the monarch's chagrin. Upon his death, it is said the King Charles asked of his underlings, 'Let not poor Nelly starve,' and though she didn't exactly starve, she did die at the woefully young age of thirty-seven in 1687.

The heady days of the true courtesan, though, were really in the 18th century when the likes of Kitty Fisher could be seen riding in fancy carriages around London providing scandalous copy for newspaper gossip columns.

So famous was Kitty that, when she fell from her horse riding in Green Park, the story hit every newspaper in town and became the subject of a well-known nursery rhyme, 'Lucy Locket'. Bizarrely, she also had a London coal barge named after her! An extravagant creature, who delighted the then-exiled Casanova with her wit and outrageous manner, Kitty was said to have eaten a one-hundred-guinea banknote in a sandwich. Her affairs with gentry and royalty were the talk of the town and she was so admired that her picture was painted by Joshua Reynolds and it hangs in the National Portrait Gallery to this day.

Courtesans whose careers were over, because their looks had faded or they had caught the pox, were known to have made fortunes from publishing salacious kiss-and-tell memoirs as far back as 1825: Harriette Wilson, Margaret Leeson and Julia Johnstone all wrote best-selling racy autobiographies around that time.

A few mistresses even captured wealthy or titled husbands by means of the threat of public exposure.

Others blackmailed ex-lovers – hence the Duke of Wellington's famous remark to Harriette Wilson upon hearing she was threatening to name him unless he paid up: 'Publish and be damned!'

One or two ladies like the vengeful Peg Plunkett just gleefully named names then hightailed it out of town with their dosh to live a quiet, sedate life in the country.

VIPs WITH STDs

Anyone sexually active can contract a sexually-transmitted disease. But since the development of penicillin, antibiotics and more recently, antiretroviral therapy, STDs are can be treated pretty effectively. 'Twas not always so. And as STDs don't discriminate, quite a number of famous people had the misfortune to catch the pox in one form or another, and for some it proved fatal.

emperors & monarchs
Herod
Tiberius
Charlemagne
Henry VIII
Ivan the Terrible
artists & composers
Franz Schubert
Ludwig von Beethoven
Paul Gauguin
political leaders & tyrants
Randolph Churchill (Winston's dad)
JFK
Benito Mussolini
Adolf Hitler

actors & musicians
Rock Hudson
Freddie Mercury
Liberace
writers, poets & dramatists
Johann Goethe
John Keats
Alexandre Dumas
August Strindberg
Oscar Wilde
also
Giovanni Casanova
Friedrich Nietzsche
Al Capone
...and quite a few popes too.

WEIRD WORLD OF SEX #6

Tiger Feat: South Korean circus acrobat, Twa Hok, was practising on the trampoline when he bounced too high and landed in the tigers' cage. A horrified witness said, 'We thought that he would be eaten, but in fact he was anally raped by the randy striped quadruped.'

Twa Hok was taken to hospital after his ordeal, but received little sympathy from the Korean Committee Against Animal Cruelty, which commented, 'If people are going to abuse animals by putting them in circuses, then they should jolly well expect to get bummed into the bargain.'